TRANSPARENCIES

POETRY BY ROBERT EDWARDS

Radio Venceremos (1990)

Nixies (1993)

A Trick of the Light (1993)

The Death of Communism (1998)

Fragments from a Graffitied Wall (1999)

American Sounds (2003)

TRANSPARENCIES

Poems *by* Robert Edwards

Preface by Scott King

Red Dragonfly Press – Minnesota – 2009

Grateful acknowledgment is made to the following magazines in which some of thes poems and prose poems in *Transparencies* first appeared, some in a previous version and/or under a different title.

Aurora, Blue Collar Review, Bold Print, Cerberus, Chaminade Literary Review, Charlotte Poetry Review, Chrysalis, Cokefish, Dakota Territory, Electric Literary Forum, Feminist Baseball, Hammers, Hudson Valley Echoes, Khepera, Lilliput Review, Mainstreeter, Minnesota Ink, North Country, Omnific, Poetry Peddler, Poetry Today, Puck & Pluck, Red Clay Quarterly, Remark, 'Scapes, Sidewalks, Swoon, The Three Seasons, Tight, Verve, Voices International, Writing On The Wall, Yammering Twits.

The author also wishes to thank the Tides Foundation whose generous support made the publication of this book possible.

ISBN: 978-1-890193-86-7

Printed in the United States of America
by BookMobile

Text typeset by Scott King in Minion Pro [9pt / 12pt]
a digital version of type designed by Robert Slimbach

Cover illustration: James Fletcher
'Invisible Presence' — pencil drawing
www.jamesfletcher.com

Published by Red Dragonfly Press
press-in-residence at the Anderson Center
P. O. Box 406
Red Wing, MN 55066

For a complete catalogue write or visit our website at:
www.reddragonflypress.org

For Patrick Stanhope

Contents

THREE: HOW TO MAKE A MAN

FOUR: DISPLACED PERSON

Preface: The Black Horse And The Golden

> ...my poetry goes
> Like two great galloping horses—
> The big black goes like the shadow of a star
> Before a lightning flash, but the golden horse
> Is like a ripple of sunlight racing across clear water.

—Hugh MacDiarmid, from 'The Kind of Poetry I Want' in *Lucky Poet*

The unnamed boy, in 'The Sisters' in James Joyce's *Dubliners*, goes to bed "puzzling his head to extract meaning from [Old Cotter's] unfinished sentences," the gaps and omissions that only hint at what may be taboo, secret, or unsayable. These unfinished sentences break off and leave listeners speechless, maybe nodding their heads out of habit, but always having to supply their own best guess at what comes next. "When children see things like that, you know, it has an effect..." Old Cotter begins to explain, then stops. In 'Wednesday's Blues,' the opening poem in *Transparencies*, the adoptee's prime mystery, the withheld and protected knowledge of their birth parents, is expressed by the unfinished sentence: "He was once somebody's little baby boy..." Not knowing, deception, and transparency define this collection of poems. Robert Edwards works to unravel some of these mysteries; he is dogged (and whaled and wolfed) by unanswered questions. And we discover, soon enough, that there is both heaven and hell to pay, as he leads us into an intractable country of un-solved and unsolvable puzzles, of houses inhabited by ghosts, of rooms hung with trick mirrors, a no-man's land of betrayals, violence, and tight lips.

Robert Edward's poems are set, often, in undisclosed locations, somewhere "between Monday and zero," "between unemployment and cornfields," or "between the prairie and the pines," making it, largely, Midwestern—think Fargo, think jack pines, lakes, and small towns, think Paul Bunyan, think gravel roads and farm fields, but then think freeway, Inter-state 94 perhaps, any road you can take far away toward survival, toward healing. A place that's "part of my Paradise— / and not a saint in it..." as Scottish poet Norman MacCaig so perfectly phrased it. *Transparencies* is a book written at some distance from that unsaintly paradise, yet even still that distance gets whispered "over and over in blue" into the poet's ear.

Voice is one of Robert Edwards' great strengths as a poet. No. Make that voices, plural. And *Transparencies* is, above all else, a book of voices, at times dazzlingly clear, at times intrigu-ingly opaque, a gathering (an intervention?) where each voice takes its turn, and each is an expert at hyperbole, impersonation, or some other Rabelaisian form of bullshit. Robert Bringhurst, in his essay 'Singing with the Frogs' in *Everywhere Being is Dancing*, desires and defends a kind of literary polyphony, where individual voices each get their say, their mes-sages and stories crisscrossing and crashing perhaps, or even ignoring each other, backs turned, but never merging into a single distinct voice. No one voice is allowed center stage. Instead, the confrontational voices, the meditative voices, the satiric and surreal and comic voices all exist on equal footing and all contribute to construct something closer to our complex reality, our lush and ragged real world, like having Hugh Mac-Diarmid's black horse and the golden (a whole herd is possible here) alive and galloping through the poems.

The title poem, with its powerfully concrete yet enigmatic images, uncannily converses with William Blake's poem 'The Crystal Cabinet,' having in common the moon, imprisonment, and the idea of transparency, transparency that is the shattering of false consciousness, fabrication, and mirrors, the pointing out of the Emperor who wears no clothes, the navigating into and out of the clouds of unknowing, transparency that is, in the legal sense, openness, communication, and accountability, and not least of all, plain old transparency that is lake water, windshields and windows, the inner sky (and the outer), the recognition of what's hidden in clear view, the seeing through to one's true, if multifaceted, self.

Scott King
Northfield, Minnesota

One for sorrow,
two for joy,
three for a girl,
four for a boy,
five for silver,
six for gold,
seven for a secret,
never to be told.

Getting Drunk On Gravel Roads

Wednesday's Blues

An apparitional howling,
like wind trapped in a nautilus,
dogs his footsteps.

A distant sound comes haunting his wake
like far surf over dunes,
or the passing of traffic in the rain:
a dream static between Monday and zero.
A sound to drown out a summer's morning.

He was once somebody's little baby boy…

But now he's a busy one, doing nothing,
listening with his entire past
to waves recall all the names of the sky.

A liquid breathing, so in time with his own,
beckons from the brine.

As if to keep
an amniotic appointment of infinite repose,
he surrenders to the lotus tide,
absolved from accomplishment.

His fingers float like autumn leaves.
The stone boat of his body
is rocked slowly toward the horizon
where clouds are miscible with their reflections.

Toward a light dreaming itself…

The sea puts its tongue in the shell of his ear
and whispers distances over
and over in blue.

Getting The News In The Kitchen

wind thin shriek
      over Susi's red phone
          the gray ford went over
      the wheel of morning upside down
          deadman's curve
into blue autumn
              black beginnings
        hands fall like leaves
    sugar and cinnamon crusted on her cheek
        someone speaking in debris
          flour dusted against an apron
    circus yellow wallpaper with white squares
    sucking winter
          from the window from her bones
              ghost motors
    where her tongue was
jack knife click
        in the receiver
      gray tone folding its oceans
    later
          john's joke
buttered over nothingness

Gunfight On N.P. Avenue, Fargo, North Dakota

Eight members of a motorcycle gang beat a man into bloody unconsciousness on the sidewalk in front of the *Pink Poodle Lounge* for challenging the pool table out of turn. Howling and weeping, the beaten man's friend drags him, head lolling on torn shoulders, to his pickup truck, wrenches down the rusted tailgate with a bang of quivering chains, and, with a tender fury, muscles his friend up and onto the bed.

Appendix scarred and tattooed Hog Mamas hootchie coo, bump and grind in his direction, mimic blowjobs with their lips and cheeks. Under a buzzing streetlight haloed with moths, the bikers smash their cigarettes out in the pooled blood, mock his tears, call him a *fag* and *rump ranger*. Tears dry on a face gone stone. He opens the door to the truck, reaches behind the seat, pulls out a rifle from its case, and fires into the air. The bikers freeze, their laughter crashing on pink neon light.

A soldier's stance—the rifle brought to shoulder, brass of spent cartridges ringing on black asphalt. The gang scatters, jumping behind motorcycles and cars, pulling .38's and .45's from under black leather, roaring curses. Shots, like axles snapped in half, like hammers on greasy steel, echo in the humid air, dopplered whine of slugs ricocheting down dark alleys. The beaten man's legs dangle over the pickup's tailgate. Bystanders kiss the sidewalk, try to crawl under their shadows or tuck themselves behind a fire hydrant or parking meter, nose to gutter grime like mother's apron. Lights come on or go out in windows above the street. Screaming comes from somewhere that might be you.

Cop cars slide together, cutting off the avenue. Tornado of red lights smear the curtained windows of the porno shop. Feet apart in a line, leaning forward, hands braced against graffitied bricks, shotguns pumped and held to long haired heads. Handcuffs lock on the wrists of cursing men shouting promises of revenge, ambulances moan to a halt. Bikers are dragged and slapped to vans. Gathering crowds, wild speculations. Second shift bars, leaking cover band golden oldies rock n' roll, empty into the aftermath, colas and beers plugged into restless faces. Statements are taken from shaking crossfire innocents. "I didn't see shit, man." Or: "I saw the whole thing."

Later, random cars, a doughnut truck, the ambient drone that passes for silence in a city, the moon sweating light between warehouses. Dried blood and bloody footprints. The avenue, glittering with broken glass, leading to a sky hot with stars and bats.

Above it all, the sound of a siren, high and thin, many brick hotels away.

The Other Breath

Someone cold is coming up the stairs. Slow,
deliberate feet. Coming,
coming. One foot
brick,

the other foot stone. He's coming
for me. I know it. I know
who it is, it's always the
oldest friend trust me so
like a brother, but I
just lie there,
frozen in the
sweaty
bed,

listening to the dark, pretending it's not happening.
One foot dream, the other foot stone. Or,
maybe, wanting it to happen dark
dark so dark wanting
not to believe
I could want
this,

pretending to count sheep. Coming /coming. Not
even trying to hide, not even
carrying a weapon, taking
both our times,
one foot
ice,

the other foot stone. He enters the room, neither
of us asking why. He stands at the foot
of the bed, listening to me breathe
as if under water. One
breath dark. The.
Other. Breath.
Stone.

Transparencies

1.

Sinistral, sister moon
phases from my blood into the fallen leaves,
into the black iron of an October wind.

The multiflorous moon goes granite
on its stalk of night.

2.

I face the prairie—or some kind of ocean—
the rind of a question mark uneaten in my hand.

Snide Madonnas total my mistakes,
bleed me with thin forgiveness, which is to say:
a dry inertia is tangled in the grass,
and I smell a dream of the darker stuff.

3.

There is a cage inside me,
with the door missing, and the sky
drapes its paws right over the threshold.

Here is where the beast
with such wonderfully clear eyes
is asleep, sprawled on dirty straw,
snoring above dark seas without wave or shore.

(Fever) (Dream) Poem

There you are
driving down the road or
just walking talking explaining
your life by breathing
impressing yourself
with futures then
like a bird flying smack
into the hard air of a window
you're cold cocked out of the
blue lying on the ground
with your big mind timeless in the leaves
and the wind knocked out of
your jokes your names for things
going black on impact
and a sky
comes out from behind the sky
checking to see if you're dead or what
and you awaken fighting breaking
your own bones to get away
from a kindness
you'll always be wild to

The Informer

It was you, old friend, and me and John, Harry and Ken. The cops followed us from the theater, but it was night black as earth and how could they know we were smoking joints as fast as I could roll them, a fat new bag of marijuana on my lap? Three days in jail, playing reservation poker for cigarettes and dark coyote laughter with young Ojibwa men or scrubbing toilets under the trustee's smirk. I was proud of my friends, who formed a circle of ignorance against the cop's frustrated probing. No one would sell me down the river.

But back on the street came the questions. How did the cops know where and when the deal was going down? No Sam Spades or Marlowes in that holster-hitching, ball-scratching troupe of small town Gestapo. They knew too many details: price and quantity, the route we'd take home. You, old friend, had arranged for John to make the buy, but in a payday mood I'd stepped in, an 11th hour backseat addition.

We wondered who the informer might be, and the compass of all the fingers swung to John, who couldn't take the innuendos, insults, threats and isolation. You, old friend, were the loudest with the logic that reasoned John into a hole. I stuck by him longer than the rest, but eventually I doubted my trust and hung my head among the pack I ran with. He filled cardboard boxes with his clothes one night and found another town to invent a past that held a future. You, old friend, always there at my side, with a reputation as the craziest and first to defy Law.

I saw John years later at a gas station. I was headed west and he was on his way back to a sideways mumble called *home*. He introduced me to his smiling wife and waved names at two kids bouncing in the backseat. He'd cut his hair, gone back to school and looked like any man you'd trust with your money. I couldn't blame the bitterness around his mouth at my clumsy apologies, his fast goodbye.

It took thick years for my daydreams to linger in the loopholes. Someone had to lie to me and for me, someone who knew I stood to lose it all, born poor with *boondocks scapegoat* written all over the dirt road I lived down. I wondered why the cops kept taking me into that windowless room and saying they knew that it was John's dope, and if I'd just sign a paper confirming that I could walk and never have to look back… I never signed, but I wondered why the cops forgot your name, again and again, old friend, and why they dropped the case when my lawyer made an issue of their memory.

The last time the subject came up, your eyes crawled into corners, and I knew.

It was you, old friend.

All the time, it was you.

Getting Drunk On Gravel Roads

It's an old sport for country boys,
something to do between unemployment
and cornfields. Show me a small town son—
before they became respectable professors
and shook their married heads at recklessness—
who didn't practice drinking and driving
with class clowns and sullen homegrown thugs.
This rattle-trap car, boony-cruising on a half
tank, in and out of calendars, on and off
the shoulder, takes us nowhere in particular,
illegal and without a map, somewhere between
the prairie and the pines. All elbows

and emptiness, we pass the bottle around.
One of us wants to drink to everyone's exile,
to something as sacred and as lost as childhood.
Another takes a slug to the death of the rainbow,
to the habits of a broken education spent
among ghosts. Still another is saying goodbye
to everything including himself. But tonight,
in the morning of our lives, we're still immortal
and don't know how lucky we are

to neither kill nor die. This road is just
a substitute for the dirt one deep inside
that will never turn to pavement or yellow brick.
It won't be the last time we try to outrun its dust,
looking for an address that lacks the proof
this bottle bears. Such belief is all we have left
of Jesus and civics lessons and algebra
we'll never use. Our words, like light slurred
from stars, arrive extinct, and all we can do
is toast the radiance of its fossilized news.

One of us tries to say that we have praised
with averted eyes those we love. Another burps
and then declares that we have stolen roses
from their earth, dreams from their pillows.
Someone makes a joke and someone warns
against it and someone else stammers over
the radio that we need to accept any forgiveness
given because we're all to blame for everything.

Take this to the bank, so say we all:
every religion is a lie and every patriot a traitor.
Trust your mother to hate you for being born
and resent you for her guilt over the hate.
Officer Friendly is a rapist with a government gun,
and the rich really think you're nothing
but a dull horse fit for a plow or a hard saddle.
Saddle by shadow, breath after breath, we
feel the old certainties die and the new truths
we wipe from our lips give answers none of us
have the courage to want. We live in a country
that was built yesterday not to outlast tomorrow.

The radio finally dies at an intersection of stars
and barbed wire, under a static of gravel under tires.
One of us says that lifting what lies in deep water
exhausts laughter, and therefore we should let go.
Another says: No, we need to hang on. We need
to find more hands. And someone else barks
Fuck You, and someone else clears his throat
and doesn't speak. We've been friends forever

for a week, losers who recognize a brother stink.
We run out of words before we run out of booze.
We park someplace called home and drive in dreams
to real lives somewhere else. This road isn't even ours.
We borrow it to get lost on, carrying its circles
under our wheels, hypnotized by what we cannot say.
Meditating assassins who have missed their targets
again, we pass dark farms, the car quiet for miles.

Yet still one of us wishes that one of us could say:
we are done waiting for some magician to arrive
with old letters in new envelopes. Now we make
ourselves into our own image and write in the sky
the names of change in our own shaky hand.
Instead, someone thinks loudly—like a whisper
of ink across a last call bar napkin:

how can we wipe the dust from the road of the mirror
and arrive at ourselves, let alone awaken
to each other and the world, when we're scared of the road
beneath the road, fearful of the hand within the hand?

Arms Of The Dark

Arms of the dark reaching out for us
like a crazy fan waiting in ambush
with compliments, sending us roses
and razors every day—

arms of the dark in blackbird sleeves,
in kid gloves, bumping
our backs, picking our pockets,
stealing the dawn from our eyes—

covert ninja arms of the dark
stalking us with a *howdy neighbor*
used car salesman foxtrap handshake—

hairy gorilla arms of the dark,
muscled with shadow,
yanking us off stools, out of our shoes,
out of our names—

lovey, dovey arms of the dark,
kissy kissy rope burns around our necks,
black and blue fingerprints
where the passion snapped—

starched arms of the dark marching us
by the ear to the blackboard
like our 8th Grade English teacher—

Sieg Christ arms of the dark,
loaded with anti-prayer,
lighting the candelabra of their hands,
saluting the night—

palsy walsy arms of the dark
around our shoulders
like a brother come home from the sea,
offering us

a smoke a toke a drink a job
under the roots sorting bones—
trusted family friend arms of the dark
beckoning us down the alley,

driving us down the dirt road,
leading us deep into the woods,
promising to show us a secret,
taking us by the hands.

Sister Sylvia

Descending angel,
                                    envoy in peach chiffon
from the planet of the debs,
                                             frog-mouthed harpy
             forking up salads
                             crunchy with bees
and rat meat fried over a Bunsen burner,
the thunder of your lost summers is a trail of poppies
foaming
             from fleeing hooves.
October children know
that fathers fall
                      from ladders everyday; life is a hell
of a lot of fun
                 until the black earth grows
            only high-heeled shoes
                         too tight
and always the wrong color
for dinner with the T. S. Elliots, the Stephen Spenders.

           Mademoiselle Baby, Mrs. Other,
playing chicken with the mirror,
Saturday night washing
                     the snakes of your hair in milk,
            your hands in Lorelei choirs—
                 the sea puts its tongue
in a rock tooth's hollow,
                        sucks at a meringue of foam,
               and never gives the moon
a chance to rest.
                 The bull straddles your bruises.
        A better fuck is Herr Death,
old friend of the family. Bad juju,
            not an occupational hazard, when murder lurks
            in iambs
            and fatal feet carry you
to dyslexic musings.
        A verdict of snow falls
            into the grave of morning,
ice sticks to your smile.
                         You drop the reins.
        Your white horse stumbles
into a blue hour.

Looking

I'm looking
for something, and I'll know it
when I see it,
so until then I'll keep looking

in imaginary diaries—
in shadows by chain link fences—
in well-stocked refrigerators—
in photographs of clouds—
in photographs of lost friends—
in old mirrors—
in the barrels of guns—
in the windows of abandoned factories—
in houses I used to live in—
in schools I used to skip—
in closets and under beds—

in homicide statistics—
in descriptions of my mother's eyes—
in that little restaurant in Medicine Hat—
in TV shows about cops, doctors & lawyers—
in motel rooms in Wyoming—
in the pockets of clothes that no longer fit—
in the pages of books that no longer fit—
in angry letters I never sent—
in the angry letters I did—
in ashtrays—
in basement boxes of souvenirs—
in the trunks of cars at the bottom of the river—
in my father's hands—
in the entire month of October—

in this poem—
           Ah...
so this little door
is where all my nightmares knock

We Are Waiting

We have the eyes of someone
who has stared through binoculars all day,
watching the fire spread,
and we are waiting

for someone to come where we are
waiting, waiting for someone,
anyone, to say something, anything,
that will lead us out of ourselves.

We are staring into our hands,
into our cups and glasses scummed
with silence. We are memorizing
corners. We are studying our listening.
We are waiting

to be specific about the flaking green paint
on the porch guard rail,
and how her pale hands pick at the knitting.
We are waiting
to be called to the long table,
to take our place and our portions
and pass the bowl on with an easy joke.
We are waiting
for the right moment to speak,
which is always long gone
and not yet arrived.
We are waiting

to introduce ourselves
to those who already know us,
to claim ourselves in their invitations.
We are listening to our waiting,
waiting for the knock and splash of a stone
dropped down a well—
one wet sound rising dark toward our dry lips.

We are picking at our waiting,
a waiting flaking away like scabs of old paint
over wood that could be new again.

We are waiting.

**My First Memory Of The Woman Everyone Said Was
  My Real Mother By Little Robbie Edwards**

running
chasing a hen through fences
brown feathers flying
my hands outstretched toward
chickenshadow zigzag running and then
a wall of legs i look up
a hand coming down
                        smack
          sitting in
the grass the
earth
        tipped over
                    spilling
out of my ear
a bee in my cheek
the one i never learned to turn

Runaways

Next to the Farm Equipment Supply is a gas station owned by a chain smoking silence of a man who drinks with the County Sheriff. His father is still waiting for him by lantern light, standing in the barn door with a whip.

He takes the keys down from their hook, locks the station early on a Sunday and drives to the cemetery, thin, cloud colored hair floating in his smoke.

He lays plastic flowers on his wife's grave, with eyes like concealed wounds reads her name in the glossy granite, dried bird shit dribbled across the dates. Spring. This would be Spring. Or early summer. No, the time of year that's both, the world changing on a wind. Shutting off the fan, turning on the heater. Waking up to lilacs glassed in thin ice. He coughs and reaches for the bottle of pills in his left coat pocket, washes them down with the bottle in his right.

His children journey maps to distant cities where other pasts are invented. They remember the nights of screaming, the broken bottle on the kitchen floor, the swinging of the light bulb at the end of its cord, the bruises they lied about to their friends, that they could not report. There are no letters home in their plans.

Acorns drop with brown thumps into the grass. Fall. It must be Fall, then. Spring was yesterday, between deliveries of diesel. A school of sparrows veer from a barbwire fence leaning its rust against a cold prairie mountain of cloud. Wind. Yes, there would be wind, leaving nothing alone. He picks up a shiny chewing gum wrapper from the grave's lush grass and absently folds it into tighter and tighter squares with his father's fingers. It is too late for everything, and the tears will not come.

He finishes the bottle at home, shuts off the TV and stands for awhile at the bottom of the stairs, his hand hovering at the *'outen the lights'* sign above the light switch. Headlights swing through the frosted windows. He goes to the door and opens it to first snow, to the Sheriff leading his oldest daughter by her elbow. She goes quietly upstairs. Next time, or eventually, she'll make it, if she has to risk a stranger to run away.

The Sheriff pulls out a bottle from his jacket, jerks his eyebrows up and down. They go downstairs, into the basement he refinished himself. The children lie awake in their beds, listening to a ragged murmur of voices float up through the laundry chute. Listening and waiting, counting the blows to come. Counting the years to go.

Blood And Water

My half-
brother,
Jonathan,
calls me on the telephone,
and we stay up late,
talking
long distance
about everything,
trying
to figure out
which half
we are.

The Fat Girl

The fat girl runs up the library steps with an armload of thick books. She passes the laughing young lovers, flawlessly fashionable and defiant with their desires. They glance up at her, then look at each other and snicker. She turns her head to hide the pimples on her chin.

Inside the library's warm, narrow silence, at a desk in the philosophy section, she squeezes her confusion in her fists. She remembers the biker who married her older sister and how he was shot by the cops in Dallas. She remembers his hairy contempt, the half pint of schnapps tucked into his black leather jacket, the way he made fun of their mother tending bar at the Spruce Goose. Her sister never returned from that summer in Des Moines. All other relatives live half a continent away and never write.

Sunlight through the angled glass scribbles rainbows across the open Swedenborg. She looks out the window and sees groups of businessmen hurrying to the appropriate restaurants for lunch. They point and chuckle at the old man who mows the cemetery grass, who throws the plastic flowers away every autumn. The old man in the baseball cap who shits his pants and smiles, who stands on a street corner and chews tobacco, watching the lights change.

Hush

Shhhh.
I'm trying to remember a dream…

floating between alarms…

       down a warm current,
           slow sugar of summer twilight…

river of faces and leaves…

…the raft
      of my sandbox
bumps up against the shore of your boots.

   *

Oh, Daddy.
I'm crying against your shirt.

I fell asleep in the dirt
and dreamed I was a man,
all growed up with nobody to play with.

I was talking to myself
in a faraway room,
and everybody I loved was dead.

The Buddy Plan

The plane home always lands at night…

The sun was shining. They were laughing at the beach. Surfer boys waxed their boards and crossed themselves knee deep in waves. Tanned girls behind shades snubbed their clumsy come-ons. They didn't care. They grinned and combed their hair too much, high-fived too much, believed in summer too much, and the sun was shining

sun screams the sky awake.

He takes the pot off the stove and throws
it against the wall, drinks the last of the bottle
and throws it against the sidewalk.
There should be more darkness than this
falling sunbright blur of mad minutes
when he remembers so much rain.
He drinks the last of the mirror and throws
himself against the world.

in their eyes. One cut himself on broken glass. Blood drizzled hot sand. One limped and said, "Give me your soldier," instead of shoulder. They looked at each other

screaming into the light.

His feet are wet again—soaked with dream:
marching in rotten boots, rain and rot,
black noise of rain on black leaves,
and no one to cover your back…

the light is the scream is the hand.

and laughed at that slip of the tongue. They went down and signed up in their swimming trunks, tracking sand over the carpet. They got drunk in the garage and listened to rock n' roll and a wind of warm rain blowing through the suburban trees. They made too many promises. They woke up without hangovers and the sun was shining.

a dust of light over even the loudest laughter.

Then (later) (again), the coffin (closed). The winter women
weeping. Inside,
so much death.
Outside
            the sun
was shining.

Before The High School Reunion

back in my hometown
back in a bar

miniskirt and party girl hair the waitress
with whom I used to play hide-and-seek
pom-pom-pullaway and baseball sets down
my cheeseburger basket and drink, says

i remember you
what are you now, a scientist?
you were always so smart

we stole her mother's cigarettes
she showed me hers i showed her mine
we leaned our heads together
in the tall grass on a hill and wished
future lives on each racing cloud

a drunken poet between jobs between
loves between
words to believe in
i make up a lie
i'm less ashamed of than my life
tell her to keep the change

between shots watching her work
jukebox lonely men for tips i wish
i knew how to reach through clouds
of smoke take her by the hand together
we'd run out the back door across
the parking lot out of our shoes our lives over
all the lost hills not stopping
until every golden oldie becomes wild silver new all

the way back
to the first wish

Weather Report

Did You Hear That?

Shaken from sleep by a dream
that slips back into my pillow,
I rise in the pre-dawn hour of birth
and death, boil water for coffee
in the cool summer station before alarm clocks.

The anxious feeling of the dream recedes
with the first hot sip, and the logic
of responsibility begins
with my face in the shadowed mirror—
listen!

There comes a cry—almost a word,
an anguished question torn between the light
and the dark. I see nothing
outside my window but the gray forms
of the earth coming into the names of color.

Now the world awakens in wheels:
round thunder of commerce rolling
past my door. Nothing human
made that sound—
unless…

    …did the cry come from me?

Weather Report

A dry mouth in a dry month
of Mondays, dust breathing at the roots.

At last—first thunder,
coming to spawn in the sunset clouds…

Later: I awaken to lightning jumping the walls,
fall back asleep to dark rain in the trees.

Driving west to work in the morning,
my shadow in such a hurry to punch in,
I see the mountains of the storm
in my rear view mirror—
a stealthy night range piled on the horizon,
its black valleys collapsing east of the sun.

Farmers must be happy
on this rainbowed morning of mud and puddles,
the wheat of the world lifted from arid earth,
and prediction of more rain on the radio.

So why do I still exhale a desert?

What sky under my skin can I seed to thunderhead?
What dance, what drum, what chant
can break the lightning from my tongue?

Old water, new water, strange
with the taste of moons evaporated from the sand—
all one to thirst,
        and hunger all the harder
the wider the wind.

The Get-Help Hotline

—One moment, please—

I'm on hold,
stretched tight into devouring time.
A faint electronic chuckling
trickles down the line: the pressure
of dark moons against my ear.
White static,
like the crisp burning of paper seas,
stays along the edge of the listening I lean into.

And I do listen, like a man at the bottom of a well,
hoping she'll return with a rope, hoping
she'll return before my helplessness
renegs on its admission.

Three clicks, snapping in my ear like a countdown.
She's back.

—May I help you?—

So much in that voice! So much fatigue
from working an overloaded switchboard jammed
with the desperate, the terrified and proud.
How her arms must ache
from opening yet another door through the mountain.
She has a stern kindness too frequently betrayed.

My rabbit silence locks itself to shadow.

—May I help you, please?—
—May I help you, please?—

I hesitate to help myself, and she hangs up,
having no time to waste on a void
when so many weep to be heard.

I sit in the dark.
I reach for the phone again.

Exceptions

Here is the mountain
from which no one has fallen.
Here is the lake
where no swimmer has drowned.

Here is the gun
that never was loaded.
Here are the toys
that have never drawn blood.

Here is the revolution unbetrayed.

Here is the poem that saved a life.

Watching The Marathon

Watching from the sidelines as the runners run:
sweat flying,
fists pumping at their hips,
ache of air over dry tongues,
a bobbing, jumping confetti river of runners,
feet slapping with a sound
like whitewater smashing over rocks,
and their *now*! eyes emptied of all *now*!
but the finish line—*now*!,
and the winner flailing in across the tape,
and the winner wobbling forward
for the handshake and the cup,
and the losers gasping in the grass…

How I envy those hearts slowing to water
sipped in shade,
those blinking eyes and faces salted by endurance,
their stretches and massages.

I almost take the breath I lost along the years,
and wish I could run,
even last,
even at the shadow of their heels,
eating the dust of their company.

Like the Chinese I wanted to brush on silk—
like the guitar whose notes fell into the corner—
like the city whose sky I wanted to taste—

Another thing I'll never do…

October Letter In Anger

Dear Magic Rat, Textbuster & Houngan of the Page:

It's true that your poetry is a blaze of marrows, seeds, continents of red glass, acidic angels. Strange, though, how easily you become bored when another is talking—unless they're famous. Why do you need to see yourself on some exalted and solitary peak, raising your name, alive with lightning, into the storm? But wait, what is this mountain made of, so unclear in all the thunder? Those aren't boulders. That's a crag of bent backs you've climbed upon. Yes, I know your genius. You inform me of it often enough—and it's true! I have never seen wounds catch on fire like yours. Nor so much water thrown on ghosts. Before I met you, I never would have believed that cream could be mixed with jade in the moon rising above the junkyards, that poems could come spinning out of the rhythms of machines. But why shake your talent like a club in my face? I have my own rainbows to carve into keys. I, too, need to sleep in trees made entirely of wind. You aren't the only one who knows the address to the house of grief. Why do you always have to be right, true Heaven tethered only to your visionary head, and why can't I have a voice to dare the nightmares, to accuse the lightmares? When you fasten your teeth into some notion of how things ought to be, you're like some grim, vein-bursting beast, and nothing, not even facts, can pry you loose. If there's any way to choke a moment before it grows a smile, I know I can count on you to put on your assassin's hands, to slip on the shadows like gloves. Yes, you're certainly behind me, one hundred percent—dropping a teacher's noose around my neck, pulling the trapdoor lever, grading my fall. I know I'm just a cockalorum, my rooster chest all puffed up with quacksalver squibbery and henhouse dawns. I know I ain't no good at museum dialects of pickled beauty, that I get my lies and lays all mixed up and speakee the Jack's English with a roughneck brogue. But I'm also the unlikely one, the X-factor in the woodpile, the one you think will never make it. My roots are clawed into granite, drinking time from the sky. Now you have stalked like a pair of scissors from my house because I dared to disagree with your latest convoluted logostortions. Get off your high horse. That nag never went in anything but circles around the same stump. The world will eat your ego soon enough. Get thy thouness gone—amscray, vamoose! This autumn light becomes you.

Thaumaturgically yours,

Widdershins Bob

P. S. — An old coat, lined with snow and hanging from a branch. The scraping of a frozen sleeve in a white wind…

Mistaken Identity

Why you

cross-eyed,
rat-haired,
pipe-nosed,
blister-faced,
bat-eared,
black-toothed,
dumpster-breathed,
elephant-bellied,
pimply-thighed,
potato-fingered,
scabby-peckered,
chicken-kneed,
dog-bodied,
razor-lipped—

oh…

It's you, old friend.

Change Of Heart

There was a time—
an angry time, a toxic time, a time of toads and mold,
when I would have wished you
fish-hook hands and an exquisitely itching asshole
and watched you improvise.

If I'd rubbed a genii awake,
or had a surprise visit from the trickster gods,
and been granted every secret vengeance,
you would've had Turret's syndrome
in lockstep with a machine gun stutter,
breath that would knock a buzzard off a shit wagon,
boils and hemorrhoids like red-hot marbles,
farts like dynamite in a sewer,

and the kind of desperate hornyness
that drives the full moon into a man's eyes
even when asleep a mile under the earth
with lids squeezed shut under a blindfold.
Rejected by everything human, you'd be caught
by the disgusted police in a motel room
full of goats and monkeys in lingerie and leather,
the black & white crime photo of the scene
clearly showing you dressed in your mother's clothes
and on top of a stiffening corpse dragged
from the coroner's slab.

There was a time
when I hawked and spit your name into the gutter
and every turd I flushed had your face.

But now, a calmer man,
a gentler man, a kinder man, a man of doves and sunshine—
I simply say:
I wouldn't piss in your mouth
to put out a fire.

Accusatory Animalia

You parrot me ferret
you ape me baboon

you fox me rabbit
you goose me loon

you crow me sparrow
you whale me rat

you hawk me chicken
you dog me cat

you badger me squirrel
you wolf me deer

you ram me sheep
you cow me steer

you swallow me worm
you flea me moose

you hog me toad
you snake me mongoose

you bear me bull
you slug me monkey

you buffalo me sloth
you duck me turkey

You & Me, Pal

for P.J.

A dark angel slumped against our futures,

something too stupid to be cruel—
like bad weather
or lousy aim drive-by crossfire bullets. Anyway,
like all storms,

he was wearing black leather and lace and riding
the thunder. One fuck away
from the DMZ,
in my barbwire bed, I watched him coming and knew

you'd be smiling.

To A Poet

You're a fucking cat,
the kind that sucks the teats of the old dun cow,
stealing my cream.

You jump up on the kitchen table,
lick the butter and jam
when you think no one is looking,
the hairs on your back as stiff as the broom
you keep one yellow eye on.

Always underfoot by ladders, spitting at my hand,
you're my best friend
when I bring home the deep-water fish.

You sit on my chest while I sleep,
and inhale my labored breath for your own.

Introduction To An Unwritten Book

Some Poems for your Delight, Kind Sir—
without Fond Hope that Conscience might Bestir
and Awaken itself from a Sleep of Thieves.

Once a Lie is told, it's quickly Married
to Two or a million, and thus is Buried
the Coroner's Shovel with the Corpse of Truth.

The Armies of Ignorance Dance and Rave,
and with Wilde Age their serious Youth would Save
from dangerous Compassions.

Believe me, good Soldier, and Be not Appalled
by men who Claim to have been Enthralled
by Ideas of Freedom Shackling their brains.

Ideas are Polished, or Filed—or Crushed.
But You must First have a Brain to be brainwashed.
So do shallow Actors Dishonor great Lines.

So many Doors to Open and Secrets to unbox,
had I Time enough and Keys, I'd open all the Locks.
A subtext Sampler, then, a Taste. For instance:

there was a Man who found a shivering Pup,
and Brought it Home and Fed it from His cup,
and Taught it Tricks until it thought It was a Man.

Full was its Belly and Cunning was Its Sleep—
until his Back was Turned, and then it Leaped!
Now it Barks over his Bones, Wagging tall Tales.

Forgive, old friend, my Rhymes and limping Wit,
and we'll Both Conspire to make a Show of it—
Heigh-ho! Down dark Elysian streets we'll Walk.

and for once you Will Listen and I Will Talk.

Enantiodromia

all the wind we exchanged
walking home in a dark dawn
from somewhere late and loud

or maybe we never left
those rented rooms
where we were always waiting for spring

i've only wanted to be happy i said
or maybe it was thunder
that moved my lips

it was raining catalpa blossoms
on the wet sidewalks or maybe
it was snowing after supper

or maybe you had torn your poems up
and thrown them
like feathers at the ceiling

we all need someone
to be amazing to
you said looking at the floor

that much
at least
i remember

Hitch Hiking After A Rain

The silent skinhead, whose St. Bernard
drooled friendship on my sleeve for 200 purple
van miles of tape recorded Hari Krishna chants,
drops me off halfway to the Big Sky,
then zigs down a damp gravel road zagging
into all the lost and unmarked Americas.

I unfurl the map
against the hands of the wind, saying,
I want to read, too.

Over there, where hope becomes a color
extracted from stone, is the road I want—
battered asphalt thinning to yarn
knotted around red hills rising
out of green hills:
thinning to a hair
where clouds squat on the mountains;
thinning to a word:
west…

Left of my elbow,
right of my thumb—
no cars.

I tap my harmonica into my palm,
bend a note for the raven
watching me from a telephone pole,
work out some walking blues
and dance the mud around.

The raven sings backup in his midnight voice,
thick hinge raucous with rust and whiskey.
The wind plays the blades of the blue stem grass.

Come on, thunder—
one more, and we've got ourselves a band!

Christmas Eve In The Mall

Who the fuck are you?—

booms the drunk by the fountain green with pennies. The Yule muzak in the mall is a neutered tape loop circling its own epic malaise. O little town of Beelzebub, with magdalen mannequins posing with a tag, this foot soldier in Harlequin's army has hair the color of old telephone poles leaning against a prairie sky. His eyes carry the sheen of a fly's thorax. Shoppers circle and bend around his glare like a current bright with fish around a mossy midstream rock. Could he be a renegade rent-a-Santa, whose odd-job Sugar Daddy lap got too cold for kiddies, who snapped with minimum wage fakery of ambient joy to the world, and so tore off the cotton avalanche of beard and wig, the pillowed pot belly. Gut slamming a half-pint devilkin of tiger piss in the men's can—and now he's Gargantua among the angels, mistaking them for flies.

What're you fuckin' lookin' at, you yaybo motherfuckers?

He just wants to be warm and drunk by the fountain he's puked in, scratch the golden apples of his balls and pretend he's the ding dong King of Candyland and these holiday halls his palace. The bottomless stein of Christian love and mercy would be extended but this bad-for-business defector from the ranks of Christmas cheer, this rogue elf and anti-Santa has made the children cry and doubt the great public bedtime story of peace among rich and poor and therefore attracted the tender solicitudes of security guards who whisper into their walkie-talkies and circle in.

Fuck you, you fuckin' bellhops!

They get him in a headlock, hustle him toward an exit, banish him from the north polis, and give him the boot and the missile-toe.

Goddamn ye nazi bastards and the blind mothers who made ye!

he bellows through a bloody nose, sitting in a parking lot snow drift. The guards laugh and cock their fingers at his head, pull imaginary triggers. He staggers up and sees a cop car turn down the service road, the blue lights twiddling but no siren yet. If he hurries, he can make the hole in the cyclone fence and lose himself behind the Char House and the Tile Emporium—and all the time, from every loudspeaker, comes a mess of bells and carols slopping over the snow. From the radio of every delivery truck unloading ooze forth glad tidings of good sales.

He brushes the snow off his ass and starts to limp toward the fence. *I'll come back in a fuckin' Cadillac someday,* he whispers to his feet, *and run you all down.*

Another One Of Those Days

Today is one of those days when everything
comes out wrong. You ask a simple question like:
How much is the bread? or *Do you have the time?*
and people look at you as if you'd sneered
at their dying mother's last request. Don't try
to explain what it was you meant because
you'll only make it worse, and the best thing you can do
is to leave as quickly as you can before
the muttering at your back gets any louder.
Take a shortcut to work and you end up lost,
the needle of your fuel gauge bumping the red line.
The police drive past you slowly at the 7-11,
talking into their radios. Ask for directions,
and you'll be detained for questioning,
have to walk a line-up, be strip-searched
and positively identified by witnesses as everyone
who committed a crime today,
your unshakable alibis met with surreal skepticism.
After reluctantly releasing you,
the cops follow you all the way to work,
letting you know they're watching you,
waiting for you to lead them to Raul.
This is one of those days when you wish
you'd called in sick and stayed in bed, waiting
for a fever. All your co-workers picked today
to quit smoking—and if you're smart,
which you won't be, you'll stay out of the Boss's way
because today you're a fuck-up and a jinx.
Machines jam under your hand
and every phone call ends in a shouting match.
And when your day is finally done
and you're the last person to walk the dark parking lot
to your car, you'll find your battery is dead,
your paint's been keyed and your tires are flat.
Don't bother to call Triple-A, your brother or a cab.
You might as well untie your shoes and walk,
and while you're at it, take the long way home.

Gi Joe Talks To The Army Psychiatrist

"I had this dream...

...Rifle ready, I walked waist deep through an over grown field, wildflowers and undisciplined grain kissing my hips. The fences of my native land had been cut or trampled long ago, and the farmers had steered their tractors under the earth.

Bees swarmed up from the blossoms, stinging my face and hands. I cursed and tried to swat them away, but my finger accidentally tightened on the trigger. My automatic shot its clip into the field—flowers, leaves, and dirt flying outward in a spastic shower, stalks hanging by a fiber. The bees whirled around my gun and then flew away into the woods.

Afraid that my shots had attracted the attention of the enemy, I dropped prone to the ground and slapped in another clip, white blood of sap dripping on my hand. I put my ear to the attacked earth. Tense among weeds, I listened to the warm afternoon...

Sudden sadness cut my occupation from me—like a death in the family, an ache of amputation. My uniform felt like someone else's, too large and clumsy, and made of fiberglass, itching in the heat.

I wanted the bees to return. I wanted to hear that *OM* in the fields, like a tuning fork of stars. Laughing hysterically, I stood up. I wanted to drag my hands through the flowers, to open the petals of my fingers for the bees to crawl over. I wanted to walk defiantly defenseless through the afternoon in a ripe aura of pollen and wings.

I shouted for the bees to come back, and dropped my gun at my feet. Tearing my uniform off, scattering the buttons like seeds, I sang at the top of my lungs, reckless in pursuit of that dwindling hum...

after that hidden honey I ran naked to taste..."

He Said

I'm getting fat and bald, he said,
and if ever the young women looked,
they don't look now.

I'm learning
to eat standing up.
I'm learning
to sleep inside my own words.

I'm becoming transparent,
an incidental weather
you stare through.

Don't look now,
but everything I say is memory.

Gothic

A dry sound in the frozen leaves
the color of burnt moonlight—
like the sound the Colonel's
starched shirt makes across his back
on the morning of the coup.

Now snow falling,
like all the unanswered prayers since tears began,
like powdered bone,
like a dead light hitting bottom,
splintered and scraped
in undertow,
and try as I might to call a spirit out of the pavement,
all that will come
is the November sound of the wind
laying its concrete cloud on the brown world.

Children, yes,
on their way to school,
forming already
their future unemployment lines at the bus.

And the weather:
a far beast approaching on a heartbeat,
pushing aside
the tall grass and buildings.

As if someone slammed
a hundred doors in my head and broke
a hundred windows.

And the weather:
leaning against my face,
inside and out.

You Never Hear The Shot That Hits You

1.

The days drip from our sides,
light bleeding through cracks into a dead sky
pinned above the chimneys.

Loneliness and buildings.

The keel of the plow plunges into morning,
turning up stones, pails full of dirty daylight,
and other celestial flotsam.

Humanity will not fit between these arms,
nor the poplar tree under its season of snow.
Somewhere, accountants are adding up
the red and black ants in separate columns, the books
in perfect order, all accounts past due.

2.

No red willow, David…

Suppose it's your birthday and the phone rings and rings…

Blood rattles at the core of silence and still
ghosts hold your hand with one lamp lit
in the other room.

3.

Poor as hell, I dig up the treasure—
and it all fits under my fingernails.

3

How To Make A Man

How To Make A Man

Someone
is always trying to make a man out of him.

In the third foster home that year
he is ordered to the garage
to by Christ learn something for a change
even if it kills him.

He tries to remember the fractions
of wrenches, engine size, make and model.
A blur of words: *tranny, drive shaft,*
differential, 30-weight, dipstick, dipshit, hopeless.
When the yelling starts,
he goes blank, waits for the blows.

Yanked up by his shirt so hard
the buttons go flying,
he knows not to put his tongue out
to taste the blood he knows is there.

Bent over a fender,
one hard hand dug into the boy's throat,
the other poised and cocked,
the man looks down at the boy's bare panting chest.

The man lets him go and backs away.
The boy slides to the oily floor, crawls
past dirty boots, pulls himself up
on a bench, careful not to touch the car.

Later, in his bed, he hears voices rising
and falling in the kitchen, wanting him out,
talking themselves into it.

The blood pounds in his head, knocking
out the old rhythm:

survive, survive, survive.

Loose Ends

The notebooks almost filled
with half-poems, stray lines—
headed for a cardboard box in the University Library
after the great poet died.

*

In the busy middle of his work
she gives him a kiss
before she leaves on an ordinary errand.
Hours when she doesn't return.
He eats supper alone,
her plate, bowl and silverware cold
at her place at the table.
Later, the call from the Police.

*

The adopted children stand
at the grave of the mother they never knew,
their gray hair lifted by the wind,
too far beyond tears to imagine
her arms hugging them home.

*

The statues to unknown gods
abandoned with their legs
still rooted in the quarry.

*

Drawers
of dusty blueprints
for all the unbuilt bridges—
the last step

never taken off paper.

The Apartment

Pictures of foreign cities tilt
like sinking ships on the blue plaster walls.
Books of philosophy and medicine bind
their remedies to the air between the broom
in the kitchen and the mirror on the door.
A gray moss of dust carpets the floor under the bed.
A litter box reeks in a corner.

The yellow cat jumps from the chipped window sill
and stretches in a hot splash of sun.
He vowels at my hand, and I speak enough Cat to know
that my legs are Mother, so I pour water
into a bowl, scoop cat food from a can.
Eat well before your trip to the Pound
because you can't come home with me…

My shadow, ambushed by morning, sits down in a chair.
This was a good man, who left his will
in park bench conversations—a man who took
his cause to be one human need at a time
and gave the world back to itself in small change
for a phone call home or bought the unemployed a beer.
Now only fingerprints relinquish the echo
of their oils to the air, and a ghost
of stink rises from underwear and socks in a pile,
his life evaporating from skid marked sheets.

The key sleeping in the irrelevant lock says
it would be a kindness to let thieves peek in
and assess this stuff that makes up the talismans
and artifacts of a life. There's nothing here
for relatives to squabble over, and if everything
were sold it wouldn't even buy a round
down the street at the bar named for a dog.
I would like to think I've plowed enough words into
the white acreage of pages to be a little wise
about the words I could've said, or say
I saw the end coming like a dawn of questions
that only now are nagging at an absence.

But I saw nothing, remember no sign or clue
that he knew more than we that he'd drop
through the bottom of a dream and wake no more.
I'm reduced to excuses and the performance
of a favor for indifferent survivors.

Was it a month ago
that his hand trembled coffee over the hardwood floor
on the way to his chair and the Sunday paper?

A week ago I would've said I cared
about so much left unfinished,
but it would have been grief for my own odds and ends
one last breath away from garbage.

When I walk in my front door I'll probably say,
"Home, at last!"

But I know it will look like no place I've ever seen.

Tired Arms

Diving at night, miles from shore.

I come up,
breaking black water,
holding the beautiful shell aloft to the moon!

But the boat has drifted far away…

Alba

Burning up with the romanticocci virus,
pushed by needling winds, we have drifted
through a zodiac of cities, arriving in each
with fewer words to translate into hope—
but still luminous with dream hydraulics,
full moons smoking in our thighs.

Viking maps carried even into sleep…

*

Ah, the hopeful years!
Every day in every way
seeing the dawn in a block of wood,
in a wheel, in faces that might be friends,
our lips tasting of sky.

One palm, drenched and spilling over with light.

One hand still stuck in stone.

*

Somewhere, a bright pen, full of birds,
will write 'morning'—
and waves will wash roses on the sand.

*

Behind, the language of dust
settles on the roads we took,
on the streets where we left
dawn bleeding through its crack
back into the earth, where we saw,
in barred pawn shop windows,
our own heralded malaise over our shoulders,

asking us, from the parked car,
"do you need a friend?"

Miles dying on the tires.

*

Why don't feet rebel, improvise
a shuffle to dance us down those streets
where we smoked our last cigarette
and spent our bus fare home?
One more last chance, that's all,
before the country turned mean,
and we began to blame the people
we should've been for never telling us
that the maps were poisoned paper,
for never returning our calls.

*

Always a step behind
or ahead,
              or so far sideways

we seem translated into our clothes.

*

Elsewhere there may be hammers
and hard light on stone.
But here are gray Tuesdays
that last for weeks,
and an apparitional drizzle on windows
saying something over and over about
forgetting, about letting ourselves run
out through our fingers, saline
or signatures trickling down
into cold autumn beds of frayed flowers.

*

Somewhere, a dull pen
is scratching along the hours—
scraps patched out of a pocket
to make the dead tree green again.

It goes to write 'morning'
and instead writes 'warning'.

*

Rising, like islands dripping with beasts,
above a dawning sea,

we open eyes still thick with stone.

Past Tense

For years,
swimming with whales,
or following strange lights and fish,

by echo
feeling my way
down cliffs of enormous night.

Years of undinal exile,
with my beard hung on coral,
playing in the depths,

anything but human.

The Last Photograph

She is watching her children look
through photograph albums of family.
She is remembering the child
she gave up for adoption, the daughter
who could be her twin.

Every smile fights its way
through documents in triplicate,
finds itself not worthy and dies
of its own light. There is always a lawyer
between her and the laundry,
between the camera lens and the vacation vista
she came thousands of miles to enjoy.

Memory is a letter
she wants to answer but keeps misplacing.
Memory is a late night phone call she dreads
will never come.

She is beautiful and avoids mirrors.
She dresses to perfection and sits in the kitchen.

She holds out a hand like a cloud
to a child who stays forever in a playground,
swinging up into the sun.

In the last photograph,
she looks away from the camera into a room
no one else can see.

Everything is just as she left it.

Writer

A man who doesn't know he has a daughter
in Poughkeepsie twists a bolt free
of rust in an auto garage in Spokane.
And where I would break a knuckle on a block,
he wipes his greasy forehead with an arm
forested with hairs like iron filings,
adjusts the trouble light and grabs
the next bolt with his wrench. But I know
his daughter is driving across Wyoming
in her first car, with his address
and phone number on the seat beside her.

Snow is falling through these lines,
melting on her windshield.
She is at that age when teenaged girls
are dreaming of the dark male angel
of their most dangerous and defiant joy.
She's run away before, climbed on the back
of a Harley and torn asphalt pages in half
on her way toward flamingo neon truckstops
where miracles are served with fries.

After work, softball and beer,
he parks the car in the garage
and sits there, staring
through the windshield, across
the ticking hood, through the wall
of years, absently worrying his keys,
remembering all the loss before,
imagining all the loss to come.

She gasses up in Idaho Falls, lets a cup
of coffee go cold at the diner.
She imagines her father a handsome pilot,
and her mother, the liar, having to eat
all those curses. She'll look into his face
and know that's where she got her jaw
and the mystery she feels in herself
will no longer have to be denied.

This is the part where you and I walk in the door,
sit down on either side of her
and buy her a good hot meal.

This is where we swap stories
and make up happy endings
for all the times we've had to turn the radio up
until the windows shake and drive
a thousand miles in our tears
back the way we came.

This is where we get drunk from an empty glass,
fill it by saying,

I'm thirsty.

Meditations In Early August

Panning for joy in the ghost towns:
Wraithville, or Spectorburg—
the stone broke and mined out vestiges
of wildcat prophecies…

Others made their money here,
so far now from the main roads.
They visit us
	nostalgically,
touch us
			archaeologically,
grateful for the distance.

Where are they now, in this desert noon,
to help us fix the doors banging in the wind?

(Young as water in a morning of friends,
the maps on our knees, the mutual frontiers…)

At day's end
we go home with a spoonful of dust,
or chip of pyrite to verify.

We dream down the road like orphans.

My Student Loan

Old hobgoblin,
pushing your warty and wrinkled cheeks
out of official stationary—
no need to be so formal.
We've known each other for at least as long
as people have been grinding wheat into bread,
or walking behind the wagons,
picking rocks from fields
where winter still sleeps in the black earth.

I carry my deceased education
in a little toy coffin on my back.
But the loan—ah!
Alive, alive-O!
And how did you get so immense?
I could tie your shoes without bending over!
What have they been feeding you
in the vaults of that far university?

I look up from the dead leaves
I keep shoveling over my shoulder
into the wind, and wonder why
your gothic shadow doesn't cool my brow.

I gather up my dust at the end of the month,
work the calculator,
return the clouds to the river.

I open up a letter, and inside is a headsman,
thoughtfully testing his ax with his thumb,
nothing personal in his professional skill.

You send me exploding Christmas cards.

Hitch Hiking To Duluth, Minnesota

On Highway 210, across the bridge from Motley, Minnesota, where I've been standing since the Ice Age, or at least an hour, with my cramped thumb out, he pulls his rig over to the gravel shoulder with an explosive hiss of brakes, crunching to a stop. I grab my backpack and swing up into the cab, tape player walking the line with Johnny Cash.

He's a tall, red haired man in a camouflaged hunting cap and vest, thermos of coffee and bottle of Maalox at his side, two silver teeth when he smiles. He tells me about his wife and three kids in Bismarck, the affair he had with the waitress in Rapid City, and the load of prairie wheat he's hauling to Duluth. I smoke cigarettes and listen, a shadow catcher by trade, silent at his need to say his life to a stranger, and too tired to share the white line lives I've invented out of an improvisational amusement to keep a drowsy driver awake.

Sway backed barns bulge from a foggy drizzle, and cattle graze in fields rolling like tightened green muscles. Clouds seem poured, like liquid granite, across the sky, or a boiling of ashes and dishwater, sliding so low they could bend the tips of pines and snag their wrack on peeling pages of paper birch. The tape ends, and he hunts the radio for the trailer court blues of a country western station but finds only static fuzzed gray as the weather. "Too much iron in this earth for good reception", he says, and so we make up our own soundtrack from the tires licking black circles from asphalt, the diesel dinosaur purr of the engine, the squeaking metronomes of the windshield wipers.

He points and I follow his finger. An old woman stands by a roadside slough, throwing bread crusts to ducks among the cattails. A woodpile is stacked against her slumping house, chronicles of tape on the windows. Discarded stoves and cars, covered with scabs of brittle rust, lean like industrial tombstones in the bushes and weeds. "Somebody's mother and nobody cares…" He half-shrugs, half-sighs.

Rocky farmland behind, the miles flying wet off his wheels—now: the crags and hills of Duluth, amphitheater city whose stage is water. He lets me off near the waterfront grain elevators, and we shake hands, shouting *so long!* over the rumble of hundreds of trucks idling in line to unload. Foreign ships nod at anchor in the center of North America, waiting to cross the inland seas of the Great Lakes, their holds heavy and golden with a harvest of prairie light.

I take it from here, walking through clouds of pigeons in the sound of foghorns, bells and gulls, ride buses with my backpack between my knees until I reach the dark street of one who's expecting me, bright lamp by the window, kettle on to boil. Falling leaves the color of cider slant through cones of yellow streetlights. A cop car slows to look me over. They can smell distance on a walking man across several prosperous neighborhoods. I smell winter on the wind.

Lament For The Lost Unknown

Everyday I lose what I've never had.
Everyday it's ahead of me, out of sight
over the next hill, or behind me,
stepping carefully in my footprints.

Sometimes I think it must be
like a ringing telephone no one can find.

Maybe if I ask total strangers
enough stupid questions
I'll realize it like a sudden smell
that jerks me back to a childhood memory,
leaving a trail of broken doors.
Then again, maybe I don't have to do
anything except sit here,
and it'll find me, like a census taker,
and jot me down.

Everyday I lose what I've never had.
It's becoming smaller and less distinct
with every hole in the calendar.
But of this I'm sure:

when all hope of finding it is lost,
that's when I'll feel it standing in my bones,
peeking around my past to watch me
from my future, from the edge of the death
I cannot imagine as my own.

Fantastique

for Janna

I pushed a wet rope up a hill.
Blindfolded and wearing greasy gloves,
I juggled nitroglycerine and rabid cats.
I held my breath and swam
underwater across the winter Atlantic.
Dressed in a sirloin suit,
I flossed the tiger's teeth
and clipped the leopard's claws.
I marched into the Generalissimo's office,
slapped him cross-eyed stuttering,
demanded that he step down,
and that free elections be held immediately.
I stopped a chain saw with my bare fingers
and picked up a car that had parked on my foot.
Dodging raindrops, I grabbed
the lightning bolt, bent it over my knee,
and straightened out the kinks.
I performed an appendectomy
on myself without anesthetic or insurance.
I went on TV and told every uncaught killer
to turn themselves in to the nearest authorities
and confess in full. And
they did.

So if I stopped you from writing poems
just by picking up my own pen,
just by insisting on my own right to dip
a bucket in the white sky of the page
and raise it up full of rocks
or rainbows—then why

shouldn't all of these deeds be as true as you?

Used

All night rolling
the stone of the moon through the sky...

Another dawn
red with headaches and the dead.

Answers no more clear
than the questions—

as vague as the faces
of those yet to die

in the beds I left behind.

Somewhere West

A local legend in this town, you never hit the Big Time and your name won't pack the house, but you're good Monday through Thursday and the gigs are there if you want them. Weekends are for the smaller towns.

You had a good ride, hombre, but it's all a business now, paychecks and weather reports. After years of waking up in motels or a sleeping bag in the back of a van, you finally made enough to buy a house on a quiet street where neighbors talk over fences. Someone leaves the band and you replace them. Divorced and mostly sober these days, your hair gone gray as concrete, you might confess over afternoon colas that the automatic mode of the music is what survives to carry every reflex expression—until a last-call scraping of chairs and rattling of glasses, and you sit to rickety applause. Flesh hanging heavy and slack on your face, you smoke and cough and read the papers. You wince when the jukebox starts up.

Some country western, some blues, and in between standard covers of the occasional moderate rocker you sneak in one or two of your own songs and a plug for your panned CD. A skinny kid from a wheat town somewhere west, you got into it for the girls, pouring your hormones into your axe, such impatience in your hands, awakening rage from a guitar with the thunder touch. You wanted to punch a hole in the sky and climb out of the eggshell blue. Driving to play a school dance, dreaming of stadiums and swimming pools full of naked blonds—while snow drifted over the road… You were on your own and finally away from your father's fists and mockery. Worrying the frets, the music so loud you couldn't smell the front row smoke, you wanted the stage so bad you would have died young to be great. You decided to survive the last time you punched a dusty motel mirror and your hand took months to heal. Between sets, you sell a few CDs, nurse your bad back, and hustle a waitress, half afraid she'll say yes.

After a Halloween show at a crossroads club, stubble fields on three sides and just over a dry county line, packing the amps into the van, a hungry kid with angry hair comes up and tells you how he is practicing until his fingers bleed, how he's got a band, some guys from high school, but they're good and they write their own songs. Chain smoking Kools in second-hand black leather, he tells you he wants to fuckin'-A dropout and take the show on the road. You bum a cigarette and tell him to stay in school, learn something like accounting and get a real job. Play for fun, if you're going to play at all, you tell him, never for the admiration of others or for money. The way he walks away you know he'll never follow your advice. He would have been in Kindergarten the first time you went into Treatment. But maybe he'll get lucky and have the talent to back it up, and maybe even live to see the last ghost leave his mirror. The world always needs another kid from somewhere west of nowhere to be The Next Big Thing.

Trucks pass, dragging a wake of fallen leaves across the road. An old wind plays the bar-
bwire. When was the last time your stiffening fingers caught on fire from a song and the
music hit you like a beautiful pain? You stand under the prairie stars with your dead art in
your hand. Your father's words return in a dust of notes. How easy it would be to abandon
everything—just disappear, like smoke marbleizing under stage lights. Become a police
statistic and a minor item on the evening news. If only you could live just one more life,
make new mistakes among new people, and live to regret new failures. A song you've
never written won't leave your head alone. You bite down on your silence. If only you
could buy a jacket's worth of wind, just walk away and be a guy, happy without hope. If

only
you could step young across the dark highway,
stick out a thumb
and ride
somewhere west, maybe, anywhere

they're not singing.

Calm After The Storm

Somebody lives in me,
at a horned address.
He has tornadoes for legs, howitzers for hands,
and a hurricane haircut.

Masked with my face,
he looks out of my eyes,
and gnashes his granite teeth at history,
grinds lightning with a stone
on the inside of my forehead.

And just when things are all handshakes
and diplomacy and I haven't alienated anyone
for a week—here he comes, exploding up my spine,
taking my tongue hostage.

He jumps into the nearest mirror,
puts up his dukes and dances
up to my defiance, bobbing and weaving,
saying, "C'mon, *Robert*, old boy,
lay one on my chin. You can do it.
You can be a *contender*."
My hand moves a hot, angry fraction—
and I'm on the floor,
red meteors slanting along my sight,
my fist bright with silvered glass.

An odor of alcohol, tobacco and riots
follows him into the bedrooms of those I love.

And now, with my one straw for a broom,
with a nail for a needle,
with water to mortar the tumbled bricks,

I go out under the idea of blue skies,
crying like a vendor, up and down the streets,

"I'm sorry,
    I'm sorry..."

Sometimes I Feel The Song Of Changes

Sometimes I feel the song of changes
has left me,
my shadow frozen to the snow.

      That's when all the books I've read
      flutter their pages like thousands of clowns
      applauding an autopsy.

Sometimes I feel the song of depths
has dried on my lips.

      That's when I go fishing for lost calendars
      in a lake of dust,
      using my tongue for bait.

Sometimes I feel the song of lovers
has ended in a fistful of cash crumpled
in the hand of a suicide, who left no note or name.

      That's when I see the blackened moon
      falling into the harbor,
      and nothing is disturbed.

Circles

He kills me again and again—stalking me, coming across the bridge I would escape over, cornering me just when I think I might make it. He has a musical koan for me, delivered at my dying. He sings it once and to the point. I wish I could describe his face. Maybe you know this dream ninja.

It's not so much death as being sent back to start from square one, maneuvering with hope over the same ground. And it's not like it doesn't hurt, the knife going in, twisting toward my heart.

Each time I get better at defending myself, stall the end a little longer. I remember: don't go that way—ambush is certain. I'm a clever little beast, learning with every last breath.

Where is he? I hear a twig snap, and suddenly I'm on my back in the grass, spitting out my blood. He's won this round again, standing over me, looking at me with impatient pity, looking at his watch. My defenses annoy him, this cowboy Zen hitman—just enough of a fight to waste his time. My sight fades on a last bubbling rattle and wheeze. He sings his riddle into my darkness.

a moon
on broken water
it ripples apart

I don't understand…

Here I am again, healed and new, staggering through swamps, lurching through thorns, looking over my shoulder. Are all these bones my own? Don't stop. Keep going. Maybe this time I'll break the game of which we're both a prisoner. If I take this rag and these smooth stones, this bark for armor…

I hear him coming through the trees, bored with my assassination.

I'll get it right. I swear I'll kill that son of a bitch or die trying. As many times as it takes.

All Your Dead Friends

You like to pretend
that you don't really want to talk about it—
well, OK, if you insist—how

one pulled a James Dean
on a dead man's curve,
and another got his big brother's gun
and painted the new white shag carpeting
the color of his parents' disappointments.

You had a list
like a directory for a necropolis,
and the stories got better with every party,
unfinished novel and poem: this one
fist fucking through the gears,
taking the blind icy corner sneering
to heavy metal rock n' roll;

or that one eating the bullet
that came back from 'Nam,
that made it through an acid sweat
Russian roulette hooch. Too cool to be lead
it had to be silver, grooved
for Charlies and bad lieutenants.

No slow motion suicide
of cigarettes and dope, decades of cheap booze—
until you check out, greasy and wheezing,
from a room full of tubes and bored nurses.
Cancer victims need not apply.

They had to be young and beautiful,
the more blood around the drain
the better. There had to be
sisters who went to pieces, cops who puked.
They made the best ghost stories.

A razor blade and a warm bubble bath,
mother's pills and daddy's scotch,
a noose knotted out of a flag and tossed
over a pipe in the school basement,
became heroic revenge against complacent age,

proof that the best ones are always buried
in the sky, legends
you can confess to when you're alone
with your reconciliations.
These myths are better than prayer
because you knew the gods personally,
their craziness explained by your survival.

And even though
you're still rising before the light,
careful in the shower
or while shaving,
or while driving patiently and without risk
on the long commute to work,
I like how you did yourself in the best:

a sheet of paper right through the heart
no doctor could diagnose,
no coroner could find.

Who's Next?

It was an uncle, and a cousin. Then,
it was your brother who used your sister
like a whore, beating her black and blue
for blowjobs. Later, it was your father
and mother, too—the whole fam damily
a pecking order of drunken raging fists
and manipulated sex, so much mutilated silence
to protect and deny. Except for you, of
course—oblivious, innocent, for years unaware…

Then it was the woman you tried to hustle
in the hospital, pressuring her to fuck you
while she was one day off the critical list.
Then it was every woman who wouldn't fetch
your slippers or fall down with legs spread in awe
of your superior intelligence and talent.

Then a professor or two, who wasn't impressed
with manifestos of your own genius. Shopkeepers
because they were shopkeepers. Entire countries.

There was the college student who confronted you
with the accusation that you had sodomized him
when he was a runaway Thorazine teenager
who had hitch hiked to you for help. To hear
you tell it, he was just some poor, deluded kid
who confused you with his brother. Then
one old friend after another who got close
enough to see the tornado twisting in debris
behind your eyes, under the well crafted ideas.
Or anyone who disagreed with you, anyone
who told you *No*. Or your sister, who tells

another story. They were all crazy. All of them.
Liars you loudly denounced with countercharges
before they could scream their secrets.

And what I want to know is,
who's next?

The Lover

He loves to say it, and the word, 'Love',
comes lush and lyrical to his lips.

He loves the sky, in all its faces.
He loves the snow and the summer heatwave.
He loves the rivers and he loves the rain
falling into the rivers, and he loves the bridges
and the boats. He loves the trees and the birds
singing in their branches, bare or green.
He loves his house and your house.
He loves fences and wind, and handmade paper,
and the rock and roll tapes lovers leave behind.
He loves the bees, oh, yes, the bees,
and the flowers. He loves praising them,
which is also a political act.

He loves the factory workers coming in after their shift
to shoot pool at the little corner bar. He loves
the waitress who brings beer to the factory workers.
He loves the young man who works at the bookstore,
and the books and the bag and the long walk home.
He loves the plumber who comes to fix the toilet.
He loves the old poet watching television,
and the taxi driver at the airport, and the divorced cop.
He loves you, too, and you can feel
the endless embrace in his smile when he says it.

Until it comes time for pretty words to stop
and actions to become a boat, a bridge, a river,
a house against the cold storm, and then he'd love

to help you but
he's never home, won't answer your letters
or your calls. But
he loves you. He does.
Really,
he does.

The Angler

It's not you. No, never you…

It's your dead Grandfather,
fishing in his aluminum canoe
before the world is awake,
the line heavy with something
that will not be hauled in
and tows him farther

and farther into the fog,

helpless to let go.

Women Laughing

for J. D.

Coming in from the kitchen,
holding the book to his chest.
Crossing his legs to explain it,
using big words, the men
somewhere, leaning against trucks,
talking about war and machines.

The circle of skirts, the looks
exchanged, their hair and whispers,
the room full of their laughter.

No longer a cute little boy,
but not yet a teenager,
he grins from face to face,
looking for some clue to the joke,
wanting to belong to their laughter.

Slowly, among the cookies and coffee,
the realization that the laughter
is at him, at his sissy weakness.
Close to tears, the shock
of their laughter knocks his joints
apart. Judged by mothers,
he leaves ashamed, the laughter
rising at his back, the joke getting better
by his leaving,
the dead book locked in his hand.

The women have succeeded.
They have given him what the men could not:
the hard look of a man.

The Hill Of Shit

for J. D.

When the therapist asked,
what was it like for you, growing up?,
you said,

We lived in a nice house,
on a beautiful farm
with a nice yard.
But behind the barn
was a heap of stumps and brush,
straw and shit, pig
and chicken heads, cattle guts
and dead dogs. When I was little,
it looked like a hill.
I remember my father
humming a hymn, the rhythm
of the pitchfork,
the piss and shit and death-smell
and the flies,
and the faint screams coming from the house.

In the winter,
the little hill would be frozen
and covered with snow,
and we'd slide
on our sleds down
the only hill we had, climbing
back up over stiff cats,
slipping on bones,
to do it all over again.

It was like that, you said.

Like that.

Naomi

            incest whispers
      hot in every leaning ear
then years later confessions to the wall
                              the window the sky
the imaginary jury in the corner

            prayers like clouds like bruises wind
   like a fist wave upon
dark wave of rage

            and then there was you
your smile
a blood-red boat on a frozen lake

                    no place to hide from so much silence
            your whole family choking it down
with Sunday supper the more alone
they thought they were the thicker the doors the louder
they stared into their hands

            and then there was you
stethoscope
   to the walls
            writing in the margins of your expensive bible
taking notes on every secret shame

thinking how
you could use it against them later

Displaced Person

To A Co-Worker

You remind me of the girl next door,
who used to stand over us in the sandbox,
hands on her hips, and boss everybody around.

In wild fields after school, or playing
hooky by the river, we imagined her grown-up:
the grim grammarian of the 4th grade—
gray warden of wayward verbs, barbwire Commandante
of the semi-colon and the prepositional phrase
on endless dusty blackboard ticking Spring afternoons,
locked and forbidden windows at our backs.
Or in a nurse's uniform someday, primly efficient
ice angel of Ward 3, twisting in the needles,
ready with enemas and cold catheters, shaking awake
exhausted patients to ask if they have slept.

(Hiding high in autumn trees, whispering
among dark leaves and laughing into our hands
as she paces below, calling our names into the cool
gloom in her best imitation-Mom beddytime yodel,
aiming acorns at her head and when she looks up
we suddenly shriek like monkeys at a leopard,
swinging down out of the moon, her sweet screams
an anarchist's payday, worth every scolding.)

Tattletale goody two shoes, practicing her masks
before a little girl's mirror, she always said
that when she grew up she'd marry a lawyer.
And she did.

She went to the right schools, made
or abandoned the right friends, sinned a little
according to the formulas of her time.

I never liked the girl next door.

What I Expect

for John C.

What do I expect from you?

I expect the sun to come up cold
and freeze my smile
while the world washes in fire.

I expect to get a kick in the ass
from an old friend
that leaves a footprint,

                and I tell myself:

after the handshake,
check for missing fingers.

That is why I really must say,
from the heart,

go fuck yourself.

(No) Common Ground

I waded these winters, ate its cloudburst hail,
swam its skies, scraped its earth
from a school of shoes,
and I claim my right to this light
ripening for a thousand miles.

By every hundred acres of corn thick with twilight,
by all the missile silos under wheat fields, I know
this prairie you've measured out
by RSVP mailboxes

is bigger than your fences,
claim-jumper deeds and titles,
your anthologies of every weed
and spiff words about its weather—

a landscape so general
its subtleties seem as obvious
as the horizons you've mined for silence.

War never comes home down your dirt roads.

Spun from the dusty glamour of tractors,
your nice poetry readings never point
a finger of accusation at the murderers of Earth
or scare your grants away by naming names
and following the money.

Pop open some wisdom in a can and hope
you know how to live by the words you pour.

You've made it hot to be a poet
who disagrees with your flat earth logic
and flatter lines,
and you own every scrap of shade between Fargo
and Medicine Hat.

But I'm too big for your shadow.

Be careful you don't get under mine.

The Ph.D. In Literature

Get three words
into a sentence and she's cut you off
again, admonishing the kids
to put down their Japanese robot toys—
Interupticons and Intercepterators,
reflex battle ready for the Monster Squad—
and find a children's classic to read,
something appropriate for their age brackets.
Once, twice, and the twentieth time
your words fizzle on the launching pad
seems a calculated coincidence
timed to keep you waiting
for her next analysis of Victorian literature,
sans Hopkins and Hardy.
The books you've read ain't got no class,
and sound too rude for dissertations.
Real poets don't come from broken prairie towns,
and you couldn't possibly be any good because
American Poetry Review has never heard of you,
because you're alive and sipping her coffee.
Open your mouth with an opinion,
and she's changed the subject.
If she asks you a question,
she'll answer it herself and be displeased
with your typical male lack of vision.
Get a word in edgewise,
and she frowns at your bad manners.
Contradict, and she complains of a cold.
Unfold a poem and she protests
of broken glasses, and so cannot listen.
Move toward the door,
and she begs you to stay, inviting you back
all the way to the car.

Hitch-Hiking To Washington State

After walking across the Golden Gate Bridge, I get a ride to Tamalpais State Park from a highway patrolman, who buys me bread, cheese, and granola, and a bottle of white wine. He shows me pictures of his family and tells me about his son, who is entering college to study botany, and about the wooden animals he carves as a hobby when he takes off his badge. As I retrieve my pack from the caged backseat, he urges me to be careful, "because there are lots of loonies and psychos on the road nowadays." Then he smiles and puts on his mirrored shades. "And stay off the Interstates."

For three days I sleep under redwoods, declining fire, ecstatic to be alone in the Jurassic gloom. At the beach, a young woman in overalls gives me tips about where other hitch-hikers stay on the Californian coast. Just when I've decided on an abandoned house with apple trees in the tangled yard, a young Chicano man walks up and offers me a ride to Eureka. "I have peanut butter sandwiches, and eggs and chorizo in tortillas in my truck." Wind in our faces, elbows out the windows, we pass my wine back and forth, washing down the good food. "Does white wine go with chorizo?" "Today it does." We pull into town late but stay up later, talking about the redwood burl tables he makes for a living, about the factory where I worked in Albuquerque. In the morning, he cooks breakfast and tries to give me money. "I know what it's like," he says, looking out the window toward the highway. "Wherever you are going, I've been there."

It takes all day to get to the Oregon border, bouncing in the greasy steel beds of pickup trucks for two mile rides, or walking on the gravelly shoulder of the highway, up one horizon and down the next. Finally, a Malibu cowboy and his peroxide bouffant wife are hooked by my thumb. I wiggle into the backseat of their Camaro, and we shout out our destinations and histories over Hank Williams's Greatest Hits and the roar of the muscle car, gargling thunder. They drop me off in Gold Beach, Oregon, then, with a wave to the tune of Merle Haggard, turn east to their mountain trailer home. I pitch my tent, invisible to the road, on a cliff above the ocean, and read Blake by flashlight, surf on one side and traffic on the other, each breaking over my shivering fatigue.

The next morning I'm up with the salty fog, crossing the bridge over the Rogue River, coffee and blackberry pie from the diner still sweet on my tongue. A heavy splash in the water below! I look over the railing at sea lions catching salmon in the river's mouth. They roll in the current, salmon writhing in their whiskers, or caress each other with their flippers. When they see me, they bark a warning to those lounging on the rocky banks. Some of them lunge yelping for the water while others look up at me and roar.

Peterbuilts and Macks honk their horns, and the drivers give me the 'thumbs up' sign. Back at ya, Gypsies. I don't mind if they don't stop. I know these Shaky Side to Dirty Side ferrymen, guzzling thermos coffee, could lose their jobs if they're caught with a passenger.

89

A rusted Lincoln Continental parts the fog and pulls over. It's an old couple, smiling and beckoning. They are very much in love. She sits next to him, like a high school girlfriend, tickling his earlobe and giggling when he shudders with pleasure. "We're going to Newport, honey," she says over her shoulder, "for our grand-daughter's wedding." "Help yourself to them oranges and that Tillamook cheese in the cooler, son," he says, shifting uphill. "I hitched all over this country once myself after The War, looking for work, getting around. I know how hungry a fella can get." We talk the fog out to sea and the bright morning up out of the highway. At a gas station, I get out to pee, and when I'm resettled in the backseat, she turns and asks, "How would you like to go to a wedding?" I sit in the back pew of the church, smiling at the cousin ushers who nervously look me over. Later, at the reception, I eat canapés and white wedding cake, and am steered arm in arm through the guests and relatives by my grandmotherly host, making introductions as I shake hands. Protesting that I should stay the night, they take me to the sunset highway, promising to return in an hour and take me home if I haven't found a ride.

In the raw dusk, a new Cadillac veers to the shoulder, spitting gravel. A haggard young businessman in a three piece suit is nodding and twitching to gear-grinding heavy metal. "I'm going as far as Tacoma," he says bitterly. "I need someone to keep me awake." I talk a fake history at him, splicing together the asphalt legends of a dozen drifters I've overheard, patching the potholes in my story with outright lies. I give him a name to call me, a credible, forgettable sound to satisfy his indifference and keep my own name clean. "Got some bucks for gas?" he asks. "After all, I *am* giving you a ride and it's cheaper than the bus." I hold out a bill and he snaps it up, not needing eyes to find money, his briefcase between us on the seat. He chain smokes and drums on his leg. My alarm clock chronicles in the dark of the car are so much audio wallpaper, and he flaps his hands impatiently at my silences. When he finally talks, he brags about his promotions, his big house and the women who come and go through its doors. Then comes a litany of all the miles of things he'd like to acquire. Later, without a word of warning, he pulls over to a Tacoma curb and says, "This is as far as I go." his face as closed as a contract that has fulfilled its cold side of the bargain and turns its signature to the wall. At a Catholic mission, a kind night clerk answers my knock, and I stretch out on a cot for a few hours, squeezed between the wheezing and farting of old winos.

At first light and after a phone call, I catch a bus to Renton where my uncle, Dave, is waiting for me. I ask for news of relatives, of births and deaths, and offer Dave my footprints, backtracking all the way to Fargo, North Dakota, and the reasons for the first step taken. He doesn't understand but accepts my need to drown a painful place in the sky behind. At last we turn into their small farm, Rhode Island Reds in their fancy chaps scattering with indignant cries before the truck. My aunt, Dorothy, home from the hospital night shift, throws her uniform over a chair, hugs me home, and plugs a pot of coffee in to perk.

I chop wood in the mornings, and watch the clouds pour across the sky and get snagged like rags on Mt. Rainier. Cattle are bellowing in their bells by the spring-fed creek, and Nubian goats, with yellow, devil-slit eyes, are leaping in their pens as Dorothy approaches with a pail. Inside the ramshackle shed, Dave is squinting under a trouble-light as he sharpens a saw. How much this place is like breathing, like a habit of hunger become a praise! I carry the wood up to the house and tumble it into the bin. I know I'm a man between two landscapes, two mothers. This is like meeting a woman whom you've seen from time to time, who after years without a name steps forward and calls you 'son'.

Sliding Scale

"You think you know so much,"
he said, taking a step closer,
narrowing his eyes.

>   *—I know—*
> said the other
> *—that someone is always leaving us.*
>
> *I know*
> *that we have the power*
> *to divert the currents of Empires,*
> *to share ourselves*
> *as fires against the cold.*
>
> *I know*
> *that our praises, like vines,*
> *drink the light from the earth—*

"You think you know so much,"
he said, taking a step back,
making a fist.

>   *—Not that I know so much—*
> the other replied
> *—but that you know so little—*

Prodigal

So you think the highway calls your name,
unrolling its risks to where the ocean
is tickling ivory thunders from black sand?

Yes, somewhere
there may be honeysuckle deliriums far
from the cold sweat of the moon slithered
in caress, where lovesweetlove asks nothing
but the fire and friction of the moment.

It's possible
that there are trees of fragrant agony
to lie under, where you can always taste
time enough on the skin of a female Jesus—
salt diva to cradle your headaches,
green eons reborn at your hands.

You think you'll leave these funny farms behind,
scorching the wired miles in a gasoline hurricane.

Your head tilts toward a thread of surf—
bullsweat roaring on the horizon.

If only her hand would leave the door.
If only you could drive beyond her vivisecting
and last words shouted at midnight and find
one mountain range of thunderous blue
they could not cross.

Out there...
    must be...
        one green valley removed
from the alkali mirages of the last chance station:

California or Atlantis, where joy arrives
pre-assembled, with batteries included,
with thighs parted and the bill paid in full.

But you'll be back,
parking your jargon by midnight
in the old neighborhood,

come to join your resignations
to these circular streets.

And how do I know this?

Because you talk too much about what you'll find.
Because you're happy as you leave.

The Bell Ringer

One foot in
front of the
other he
climbs the tower to
ring the
bell.

Each day the tower
gets shorter, but the climb
gets longer. It's a mile if it's a meter.

Even the bell is shrinking.
He drags his life up the steps to pull the rope
and yank a tinkle
from this dusty toy.

He's too tired to brag
about how he used to run up the steps each day,
breaking through the clouds to ring the bell,
the thunder of its light rippling over the world,
again and again and again.

Yawning over his job,
he plans his next nap.

He will dream that the full moon is a bell,
and he pulls the long, black rope,
pulls and pulls,
the silver surf
of its ringing announcing
the end, the beginning
of the world.

Blue Friend Ghazal

I will sweep the dust behind the door, my friend.
I will sleep with the dust no more, my friend.

Ceilings are at my feet. My ears wear shoes.
When did you stop being my friend?

Bees make honey from the foxglove—I dare you
to taste it. How did you stop being my friend?

Rewards are another word for dust to the lonely.
Why did you stop being my friend?

Robber Deadwords, go to the dusty mirror, stick out
your hand and say, *Pleased to meet me, my friend.*

Christmas With The Relatives

All afternoon I've sat in polite company, a sawdust Orpheus poxed by twinkle lights constellating the artificial tree. I've held my tongue with both hands, smiling through clenched teeth at opinion served up like pastries by fluffy aunts who buzz back and forth about recipes for fruitcake, the assassination of John F. Kennedy (the commies did it), and how Jesus loves us so much He wants America to put a bullet right between the eyes of the world. The sky is green here and oceans flow backwards to the clouds. Freedom is a chain of churches and malls. Justice is a crossword that intersects with rust.

In their respective corners are men chewing silence, or if they speak, it is to suspiciously swap axe-knowledge, blade-lore, engine-cunning. You could kill men like this with a sudden hug, or drive them out in pickup trucks to dare the snow drifting over roads. Good Lord, give these men a tool and something to fix before they're forced to prowl knickknack shelves for books or ask the television why it lies.

Fists of Bibles and sermons of ice cream, screaming children chasing each other up and down the stairs, reminiscences about those who have *passed on*. Legions I am beginning to envy… What have I done that I am sentenced to 25 White Christmas Favorites playing over and over again? Hark, I swear on the grave of Bing Crosby this just might be the Holly, Jolly Christmas where I put that little drummer boy out of my misery, and no jury south of the North Pole would convict me.

Uncles, aunts, cousins and their spouses: they've given themselves the missionary gift of feeling Christian and charitable by pretending for a few frozen hours I am family. I'm a corner-of-the-eye creature, a loser-in-law, food for whispers. They've heard rumors of poetry and worse. I think they can tell their God gives me hives, their flag the heebie-jeebies. Myth is an easy substitute for history and goes better with gravy. It must be nature because nurture could never create such an alien stink as I wear for cultural cologne. They welcome me as they wish me gone, and both of us regret my fork in their pie. I'm the weird kid who confirmed their convictions that little bastards grow up angry and ungrateful for the crumbs they're given. I'll rip the shiny wrapping from an imaginary box and open up a world where I belong. If there were civil war, they'd give a Rebel Yell and I'd be the first one they would shoot.

Now it is silent night and I've given my address again and again to those who will never visit because there are no gun or quilt shows where I live. Thermometer mercury curls into a little ball and raw solstice leans on insulated doors I don't need Rudolf to help me find.

Sweet Jesus of Joe Hill and Mother Jones, how good it feels to walk out into the December air, cock up a leg, and blow an ass ripper of a fart to the north wind!

Observation While Listening To Charlie Parker

I think that my sweet relatives
would cross a thousand mountains
to wipe away a stranger's tear,

but wouldn't ford
an empty street on a green light
to hand me back my severed arm.

I think that my sweet relatives
would cross a thousand mountains

The Mud Lake, Minnesota, Poetry Reading And Church Social

Notebooks and potato salad, manuscripts and meatloaf, sonnets and balled up tissues pulled out of apron pockets. A token howl of feedback from the microphone—something to cue the wolves—and the Reading begins…

One of the Mad Poeti is reading from *The Beatitude of Babies.* The curtained words wobble apart to reveal a rosemalled heaven of cribs in golden rockabye Sunday afternoons and first words. It's a given there's no baby shit at 4 a.m., or the temper tears of toddlers stamping their feet No! No! No! Fifteen poems to Jesus, five times as many as nails, because the red and wicked world is jumping and twitching in the heat of its own death and happy to be burning and needs to be poemed and prodded to the hickory switch of our Savior. And now come couplets in true red, white and blue. Town ladies and farm ladies get this tingling in their Deuteronomy when the flag goes up the pole!

The Catholics have their bingo and their statue of Mary in a washing machine surrounded by flowers (Our Lady Of The Kelvinator, O Virgin Of The Westinghouse, Mother Of Whirlpools—wash, rinse and spin our sins away!). The Baptists have their choir and their whiskey in the barn, and the Methodists have preachers with degrees and pews waxed to a slippery gloss. These gray haired grand dames have all done the tour of the Great Museums of Minneapolis and know there is nothing better than potluck and rhymes in the basement of *Our Lord O'The Lakes Lutheran Church.* Pastor Jim Gunderson knows he'd better lend a hand with the paper plates or else the ladies will be mighty miffed.

If only we could hear odes to casseroles and fresh laundry on the line, go walking beans with the scansion of a hoe or hear a prosody of peas with butter yellow as dandelions in July, a counting of beets per measure. Fast forward to canning time, go down to cellars and count jars dark with pickles, tomatoes red as showroom tractors, edible bullion of corn. Farm accidents and shirts they sew for one armed sons, daughters who keep trying to come home, husbands growing strange by trouble light.

No, these women of Mud Lake will stay ladies in our time, but they have gifts of labor and endurance I wish that they would celebrate and share. I know these women, who know working in the rain, who get up before even dreams of warm milk and watch deer cross fields green with knee-deep corn. I wish they would come with loaves of poems as high as their white bread comes from the oven.

One by one they leave modest houses, go down to the riverside and are laid under flowers, in American earth, their clans singing above them, embarrassed by grief, forgetting their recipes. Yet their eyes and smiles are alive in wild little girls reading books in trees, chocolate on their chins.

Lines

Do you remember
sitting in a chair and falling
off the edge of the world?

It was the year
when we were always passing something
hand to mouth.

You reached past me
with a bandage on your hand
to change the station on the radio.

It was the year
when we were always sweeping
up glass in the morning.

Do you remember
letting go of the chair
like you'd let go of an airplane?

Falling,
         falling,
                  falling…

…toward snow or a pillow or the page.

I reached for you
like a parachute,
like an anvil,
but my hands were full of static.

It was just you and me and the moon.

All falling together.

Sally, Sally…

There you are, Sally, burning horizons on your wheels again, breaking out of the ramp and the weekend city, changing lanes on the Interstate like a pro, flipping off the honking truckers wagging their tongues at your rear view mirror.

The last suburbs march their berms up to barbwire marking farms for sale when you exit onto the two-lane tars, skunk scent clotted with fog for a moment over a bridge. But you have Friday miles of twilight on your tires, navigating by habit, before you turn by reflex down gravel roads walled with corn, night thickening among the stalks, and can shut the radio off at last and let the dust of home pour in.

This is how it should be: Lynn walking under dark trees, shivering from the river, shaking the current from her hair. Todd should be making a birch bark mask, like he used to do, barefoot and listening to owls. Dishes will be done, the sheets thrown into place just enough to know they made love before supper.

But this is how it will be: a rusted truck outside of a trailer house on blocks, and the skinny black Labrador rising to bark from a pile of carpet remnants. Todd will turn over for one more shard of a dream before his part-time job as a night janitor. When he's gone, Lynn will cry, her red elbows on the Formica table top. She's pregnant again and wants to keep it this time but the hardware store is closing and she was pink-slipped last Monday. She'll drink too much, because what-the-hell, and you'll help her to bed again because she is your cousin, take off her shoes and smooth away the sweaty and bacon-scented hair from her face.

Practical Sally, shrewd and methodical, you left all this to go to school and get a good job as a nurse. It could've been you down a dirt road in a trailer house painted headache green or boredom beige. It could've been you shutting off the TV, listening to swampsong of frogs outside of any little town failing store by store. Your eyes following the tail lights of the lucky ones through the corn and up into an endless boulevard of stars.

The pump handle creaks and you drink from your hands. Last night you checked the doors and windows, checked the pistol under the lamp, turned off the lights to sirens, then laid awake listening to the couple in the next apartment get drunk, argue, smash things. Later, their bed squeaking on the other side of your wall. You thought about how good the water used to taste, how you'd lean against the kitchen counter and sip the liquid light, pretending it was wine. The sound of distant traffic on the freeway sounds like pines sieving the breeze for fireflies. Headlights in your mirror, trucks banging over manholes, might be tractors harvesting the dark in late fields.

But here, breathing the air that will always be home, in the place you return to every chance you get, you can't wait to leave.

Her Dream

I dreamed
>there was a storm coming:
>dark, rolling clouds,
>thunder
>like the end of the world.

>Children were playing in the yard.
>They broke up their games
>and ran. Fear
>rose with the wind.

I dreamed
>that you were coming home.

Old Hippy

Scarves and guitars,
honey and herbs,
an axe in the woodpile
next to the fieldstone house,
goats leaping in the pen
while the pipe is passed…

For the time it takes the moon
to climb down
and up
the fire escapes
and cross the alley,
he remembers these things,

his piss cold in his pants,
the bottle empty beside the dumpster
he leans his head against—

                    a painted van
flowering with music:

greasy air conditioner raga

closing his eyes,
filling his bones
and gray beard

with the light of lost summers,

his hands closing around the smoke
of lost hands.

Lilacs

Because the blooming lilacs spill
the purple ghost of their scent
on the jacket weather of the night,
and the May moon is swollen with a glow
stolen from foxfire,
and every myth assumes a believable skin,
I walk whistling down the alley
toward the hill above the freight yards
to watch the boxcars, squeaking
over greasy steel, take on
a shuddering load of Midwestern shadows
for all points east or west.

The blackened alley scatters on a backyard light,
and a young women with a Doberman on a leash
suddenly sees me just as I see her.
Why she didn't hear my clumsy
birdsong blues, I don't know, but fear
stiffens her stride, and the dog growls,
teeth all the way to his tail.
Lard hardens cold around my heart,
and for an immense moment, I think
in fast forward that she'll drop the chain
and give the command to attack,
her precautions ignited by surprise
into a panicked assault in defense
of her right not to be a victim and be free
to walk the darkened city where and when
she wills. *Me, too,* the wrong man thinks,
and licks a broken note from dry lips.

Ready to run with jellied knees,
I keep walking, faking cool
indifference, and look away toward lilacs
to demonstrate that I know how
to keep to my own side of things.
No words of trust or comfort are possible,
and the dog stays on his leash—
just a blade of fear passing between us,
no gesture so important as disinterest,

so that we can invent the night
for ourselves and proceed in peace
to buy a quart of milk, or walk the dog,
or watch the moon rise over the boxcars
in the smell of lilacs on a hill.

Grandma

Grandma, I am opening doors to empty rooms.

I am descending dark stairways to subterranean balconies crowded with the violets of your voice…

Old woman, with your purse full of pennies, your bruises from bread, your broom of despair, reproach me for flying off the handle, for not forgiving certain humiliations imbedded in my stride. I'm sorry that I ask so many questions and hide in the woods, that I'm lazy and always pulling tails.

Mother to so many, mother by reflex, your suffering eyes rise through my own, trying to see if I grew up to be a good man.

Mondays of clean burdens on the cross of the clothesline—baptisms for the sins of underwear and sheets. You loved us all under the weight of pure white, loved us in advance, breakfast by supper, ready with the coffee and grandpa's boots, confessional with attics and photograph albums.

A garden overgrown with weeds…

You stand with the grief of your chin in the quarter moon, unable to clear a row.

Grandma, I am opening doors to the other side of the world, but I'm afraid that I'll never get to be anybody's son. I'm afraid I'll have to stay like this, holding out my arms to the north wind, addressing the dead.

And it's far too midnight for that.

At The Last Minute

A few impressions before I go:

portable prisons
that even allow me to go through doors,
to make love.
The scratching of itches so deep
that ferns get under my fingernails.

An old friend tells me,
"you look like a man who has lost something—
maybe a pair of glasses overboard at night."

Yes…

   The boat rocking on water dangerous and deep,
my eyes wide and unfocused
     staring like the dead,
         or squinting at blurs—

   I really don't know
which is the way to shore,
    which is the way to the dark,

       open sea.

The Factory

I can't remember—what is it
that we're making here?

Conveyor belts march boxes
toward the loading docks, earthquake
of machines, bright lights and busy busy
men & women.

And the money's good, the Union strong,
production's up. *Your attention,*
please, the loudspeaker announces—
promotions for everyone!

But what is it
we're making here?
Why can't we see
what we're making here?

Why, when our shift is done,
do we weep like the grieving
at our kitchen tables,

as if something we cannot name
is gone—not just lost from our lives,
but from seasons of earth itself,
leaving not even a legend behind,
and we weep and rock and hold
ourselves under the dying sky,
wanting to give ourselves completely
away to anything and enter

Swedenborg's dream
where something 'holy and indescribable'
shook him, threw him to the ground
and forced him to pray.

Transfer

back & forth on the bus
work/home traffic mantra
a routine built into the blood
dead windows nose in a book
turning pages turning corners
knowing by any weather's light
when we've crossed Goodhue
when we're on Fort Road
passing the funeral homes
pizza joints antique stores
or St. Clair the sound
of the engine speaking hill
enough time to finish the page

until laid off

but going that way again
months after the anger
something i never read
in the lost light
colder now between the lines
noticing every stop i had forgotten
in the reflex
river of the moment
counting how many new faces
in the old seats

Hard Copy

A metronome of rain water drips
from rusty fire escapes:
a night dismal with coal trains
and barking dogs.

In an alley,
a taxi driver takes a drag from his cigarette
and watches the moon riding
the skyscrapers
as if he were looking into an apartment window
where a woman is undressing.

A middle-aged couple
shout at each other in the taxi's exhaust fumes,
red taillights smeared on their faces,
a broken bottle of gin at their feet.

Drunk or sober,
in beauty or despair,
under oracular skies or under
a piss-colored moon—

the meter is still running.

Accusing The Moon

O moon,
you wear me out.

I'm a live wire
carrying the warm oil
of your current.
I arc blue screams
to everything I pass.

Your light digs a grave
in my forehead.

Your light butters the rust
on all the abandoned cars
I want to drive over the ocean.

Your faces all look down
their noses at me.

Moon, hear me out.
I can't take much more of this.
You come with your scythes of light
and cut my grain down green.

You make me say goodbye
to everything I love

by introducing me to it.

Wherever The Lightning Is

Horses are grazing
around old and broken farm machines
abandoned in the weeds.

They switch and swish
their frayed tails, twitch
and shiver off flies, cock an ear
toward wind leaping
from milkweed to thistle.

Thunder falls
down a mountain of prairie cloud,
rolls and breaks
into a funeral bloom of crows,
leaving a windbreak of dead trees.

The first hot drops arrive
on a dark smell of earth.

The ocean returns far inland,
its one endless wave crashing through the sky,
hurled beyond salt.

Heads lowered under the storm,
the horses cross the sudden pasture creek,
turn their backs
to the stinging wind,
and nuzzle each other under fenceline maples.

Wherever the lightning is,
you and I are not in this poem.

We never were.

The End

New heroes in the stars, old warnings
in the bones, a judgment in a rainbow
skin of oil on a river. Houses turn
inside out. Discard your fossil dictionaries!
What is dead shall live! Let the earth
speak! Let everyone awaken
from the long sleep of the sky! Be amazed!
Be afraid. It is the end of the world,
and everything you know is useless.

*

Nostalgic for the future, we thought we heard
this music before, shaking the walls.
But it was only the wind blowing the shadows around,
coming Long Distance with an artificial voice
intoning a bland demand for more money.

*

Like fish seen dimly swimming at the bottom of a pool—
dark moving within the dark: a dream that millions
toss and turn to, crying out with tongues thick
as animals taught to say, "I love you!" and "No!"

*

A man who might have once turned over
the Hanging Man and smiled with hope,
who might have once seen Winter
as the herald of Spring, has painted
his daughter's bedroom door black.
He drinks all night on the porch
and smashes the empties in the grass.

A convenience store clerk, mother of three,
shot execution-style for $150. Paper knives,
signed by judges, slip along the wound of silence.

It is the Day Of The Investor and the old night of the gun.

*

Give us a sign, the People cry, a wave
red with fire—something official that says
we are on the threshold of a prophecy fulfilled.

*

Was it in 30 or 60 A.D.? Or in 90,
when Saint Clement I predicted the end
of the world at any moment? Or was it
in 500, or 1000, or 1284 when Pope
Innocent III added 666 years
onto the date Islam was founded
and discovered the sum to be Apocalypse?
(And yet another final year was 1669
when 20,000 of The Old Believers in Russia
burned themselves to death to escape the Anti-Christ.)

On October 22, 1844,
Seventh Day Adventists gathered on a hill
to await the meticulously calculated arrival
of the Coming Of The Lord and the sky sing with light.

And waited. They sang every song twice.
Men cleared their throats. Women coughed.
Children excused themselves to pee.
It got dark. Everyone was hungry. They went home.
They went back to work.

*

It is the hour of drowned sailors,
when the lid of the harbor closes
over the objections of the shore police.
It is the hour when bag ladies stand in alleys
and chew their gnarled knuckles. It is the hour
when Hominy John has a heart attack while sleeping
on a grate and the sidewalk crowd steps over him.
The junkies weep for him and themselves
as they go through his pockets.

114

                              *

In 1999, I placed an ad in the paper to sell a truck
and a woman called my number to tell me
there would be nowhere to drive after the year 2000,
no gas, no roads. That will be the year,
she said, when white people take back America
for Jesus, whose face they will see
in their crashing computers.
The signs are clear.
Stock up on firewood, she said.
Buy guns.

                              *

As if the future is hidden in the past,
a labyrinth that leads us back to our beginning,
which was another kind of end. As if
God whispered hidden holy clues
and they sounded for centuries like leaves
falling, like the distant wind of a storm
coming and only those detectives blessed
with spiritual ears could bend
close enough to hear destiny's echoes.

Fate, then. Inescapable. A Doom,
laid like a shadow on the world. Not
a sniper's bullet or a car bomb or a missile
under a cornfield. Not an asteroid blazing
out of a beautiful blue sky, a super-volcano
under the sidewalk, sunspots, magnetic
field reversals, a virus like a curse. Call it
anything you want and twist a verse
as evidence planted to frame, but never call it

being victims of our own stubborn stupidity, never
a twitch and tick of the universe: a simple trust
of light and gravity and beating hearts
betrayed by what we never believe possible—
angina or ice age—until history
becomes archeology.

*

A hand, coming out of the dark,
open as if to say, "Stop!"...

*

Should the Age of the Jaguar end
on December 21, 2012 AD, in the fifth
and final sun, during 4 Ahau 3 Kankin,
ruled by the Ninth Lord of the Night,
and only the usual and mundane terror
and insanities occur, then I predict

the reincarnated end of the world
will be given fresh letters of introduction,
by Rapturists and Revelationists,
by politicians with new enemies to invent,
by astrologers, prophets, seers, soothsayers,
and those putting words in the dead mouth
of Nostradamus. In other words:
the usual suspects peddling the usual fear.

*

A drunk in the gutter. A little boy wiping
a bloody nose. Beggars, bastards,
the exhausted poor. Or the fine citizens
cowering within the church of their secrets,
and murderers who want to be caught:
all those who would burn
the world down with a snap of their fingers
for a second chance. Oh, how they pray
with rage to the starriest part
of themselves

that a butchery of dawn redden the sky.
And when fire is washed from the newborn skin
of the mirror, everything broken
will heal, every tick of the clock
be a kiss, and the simplest,
sweetest thing will become clear:
love.

                    *

It is, it could be, might be the hour
when magnificent significance is revealed
in a shadow on a bridge.

Or was it someone falling
out of a life?

                         *

A jester with tin bells, a painted clown,
masked as myth or a criminal, a dangerous doofus,
classical and grotesque, deadpan creepy
and infected with ridiculosis,
reads in an exaggerated thespian tone from a long list
of Xanadus and Xanadon'ts.

Performance art, if you will, except,
in this case, the hostage audience is naked.

Then he giggles and juggles
sugar skulls and sacred texts and sings
out of key in a high, squeaky voice:

everyone was looking so hard
between the lines
they forgot to read the lines.

                         *

No bang. No whimper. No Hallelujah dawn.
No Kachinas dance. No number ablaze in the sky.

Just one day you're standing at the window
with a cup of coffee.
A calendar in the blood flips over,
and something in the light says:

be afraid. Be amazed. You are in the new world.

Insomnia Because It's Tuesday

All night rolling the stone of the moon through the sky…

Ghosts shake my hand.

> *Congratulations,*
> *well done,*
> *and Good Morning!*
>
> *You made it this far*
> *with only second-hand light,*
> *now close your eyes*
> *and sleep.*

All night rolling the stone of the moon through the sky…

Listen

I dreamed I was in a race…

Bang! goes the gun—off I go!
I shoot glances left and right
to size up the competition:
no one. I'm alone. I'm running away
from the dark, toward the dark,
the road invented one step before my feet.

I ran for years all night

and woke up tired with a start
at the finish line before the dawn.
Bang! goes the gun of the clock.
All winds travel in circles,
falling from the horizon
ahead or behind. That's what the boy

inside the man inside the grandfather
bent inside of me yelled across the river
of sleep to my waking name.

(At least, that's what the echoes said.)
I whispered back, across that dusty ditch:
give me wisdoms I can use.

An immense minute ago
I was sitting at my desk made from a door,
writing to the you of I in the green
smell of summer. Now I'm sitting
in my theoretical garden, talking to paper
while real snow drifts
against my imaginary feet.

And before my breath leaves these words,

I want to end this by saying
what matters to me, as if a dying man
should grab the hand of any passing stranger
and gasp out his life story.
I want you to know the reasons

why I dance with arms folded and laugh
with a frown, why I am a tree that dreams
of travel. I want to stop
making excuses for being innocent,
for hiding behind the plutonium in my bones
and offering a refracted honesty.

I don't want to live in the little spaceship
of my words, orbiting a dead chunk of heart.

I want to write poems that carry everyone,
in the way each river carries the moon
in the circle of its arms,
even under the ice. Listen,
you can hear that cold liquid light,
running out of the dark, toward the dark,
flowing over stones…

They're like words someone needs to say,
as if they were the last thing they *could* say,
just before the end of the world.

Displaced Person

The blurred years...
Nights of whiskey stars...

Where was I
to have gathered so much winter?
What earthquake did I ride
that my hands shake so much?

The wolf was loose!
The wind chased him through the house,
tipping the grease into the fire,
fanning the flames so high
they scorched the moon.

Interior tectonic wreckages seen orbital
from a chair, high on Damitol,
drinking my Lethe from an old fruit jar.

Shadows of smoke drifting across snow
in the cold cities I staggered through.

And then, all this rubble—
the blow over,
the factories of lies now full
of sky, lead
dust of a powdered world settling in my hair,
on the coat I stole from the dead.

Now I'm up early, with smoke
in my clothes,
cleaning old mortar from bricks,
stacking them in rows,
clearing the foundations for joy.

I stay up late, polishing the moon
with my sleeve.

Waiting to leave,
whistling among the ruins.